WELLAND PUBLIC LIBRARY

# CATCHING AIR

# CATCHING AIR

The Excitement and Daring of
Individual Action Sports—
Snowboarding, Skateboarding,
BMX Biking, In-Line Skating

## Bill Gutman
## and Shawn Frederick

CITADEL PRESS
Kensington Publishing Corp.
www.kensingtonbooks.com

CITADEL PRESS BOOKS are published by

Kensington Publishing Corp.
850 Third Avenue
New York, NY 10022

All Kensington titles, imprints, and distributed lines are available at special quantity discounts for bulk purchases for sales promotions, premiums, fund-raising, educational, or institutional use. Special book excerpts or customized printings can also be created to fit specific needs. For details, write or phone the office of the Kensington special sales manager: Kensington Publishing Corp., 850 Third Avenue, New York, NY 10022, attn: Special Sales Department; phone 1-800-221-2647.

First printing: January 2004

10   9   8   7   6   5   4   3   2   1

Printed in the United States of America

Designed by Leonard Telesca

Library of Congress Control Number: 2003106186

ISBN 0-8065-2540-1

# Contents

## PART FOUR: IN-LINE SKATING

# Introduction

They jump and soar through the air, ride down rails, fly out of a half-pipe and off a ramp, doing amazing and dangerous tricks before landing, and they love every minute of it. These are the incredible athletes who now participate and compete in the rapidly growing sports of snowboarding, skateboarding, BMX (bicycle motocross) biking, and in-line skating. At one time, these were euphemistically referred to as *extreme* sports, a description considered overused and outdated by today's athletes, who no longer consider such feats "extreme." In the eyes of those who watch them, however, these athletes are doing some of the most amazing things in the sports world today.

There have been other descriptive words of reference as well—*alternative sports, high-risk sports,* even *outlaw* or *rebel sports.* In today's world, however, their surging popularity among the millions of young athletes who practice them makes them simply one part of the overall landscape that is just plain twenty-first century sports.

There is, however, a major difference between these exciting and high-flying sports and traditional sporting fare. While such iconic American games as baseball, basketball, and football emphasize *team,* snowboarding, skateboarding, BMX biking, and in-line skating recognize the *individual.* In fact, they are purely individual sports, where each athlete has a chance to show his or her creativity, daring, skills, bravado, and originality, and which can be displayed either in an organized contest, out on the street, or in a skate park, where young athletes work on their own to devise new tricks and ways to merge body and board, bike, or skates as one.

However, it wasn't always this way. It took many years, and the perseverance of many young athletes who wouldn't quit, for their sports to achieve mainstream acceptance. There were times in the 1970s and 1980s when all four of these activities were considered fringe sports, and were a pain in the derrière of the general population because skateboarders, in-line skaters, and BMX bike riders often used the streets, sidewalks, and parking lots. Few places were specifically set aside for them, and there came to be a perception that these were sports practiced by young people who wanted to rebel, who were out of the mainstream of team sports, and maybe even out of control. It was even thought that one of the sports—skateboarding—was an unhealthy outlet practiced by kids headed for trouble. The image was bad and, truthfully, some of the young athletes loved that.

Snowboarding, of course, is closely related to skiing and, at the beginning, that was one of the problems. Most ski resorts felt that the slopes could not be safely shared by skiers—who tended to run a straight line, top to bottom, on a hill—and snowboarders, who loved to carve side to side as they made their way downhill. That conflict often led to collisions and near collisions, making most hills off-limits to the snowboarders. Tradition came first. Today, all major ski resorts set aside separate areas for snowboarders.

In the early days, snowboarders were forced to ride out of bounds, off the beaten path. Boarders often hiked through deep snow to their own sections of a mountain, then rode the natural terrain, slowly developing a freestyle form of the sport—riding over and around obstacles, dodging trees, jumping off rocks, and developing tricks—that would endure, even after the resorts opened up their slopes to snowboarders. Later, the sport would also emulate skateboarding as riders entered the half-pipe, going up a wall of snow and into the air, to do a series of incredible tricks that evolved directly from the sister sport, where the half-pipe was already an existing discipline.

Skateboarding has had an even more checkered history, enduring more ups and downs than a roller coaster. When the sport's popularity first began to grow in the mid–1970s skateboard parks began springing up all over. Soon, however, they were forced to close because of insurance problems and questions of liability when skaters were injured, as well as lawsuits and the threat of lawsuits. That's when the kids who loved to skate were forced to take their boards to the streets and a whole new style of the sport evolved. At the same time, town officials and pedestrians alike began to view skateboarders as troublemakers who had little regard for either property or people. They would skate anywhere, with any kind of public property becoming an object to jump over or ride on. And, of course, there were inevitable collisions on public streets and sidewalks, with both pedestrians and automobiles.

By this time, skateboarding was considered an outlaw sport. People perceived the street skaters as different in a negative way, kids who wore strange kinds of clothing—baggy pants, t-shirts with all kinds of strange images, such as symbols like the skull-and-crossbones—that their own kids wouldn't wear. Because of this, many felt the sport would die. But it didn't. Before long, skateboarders discovered the joys of riding in the half-pipe, and innovators such as Tony Hawk came along to do amazing midair tricks that turned on a whole new generation. When it became possible to build skate parks under hazardous-activity laws that made unnecessary the need for liability insurance, the sport was back to stay and heading for the mainstream. This law, passed first by California in 1997 and later by other states, "made the construction of all public city-owned skateparks . . . possible by officially listing skateboarding as a hazardous recreational activity and freeing cities of liability." Similar laws have allowed the sport, as well as other action sports, to grow and prosper because the proliferation of parks and other legal venues has given young athletes more places to practice and have fun.

BMX biking, though it never enjoyed the widespread popularity of skateboarding (apart from all the young people who rode BMX bikes strictly for recreation) followed a similar path. BMX riders who considered what they did as sport really had to find their way. Eventually they, too, began to do tricks on their bikes, right out on the streets. In fact, while the most spectacular aspect of BMXing today might be *vert*, the term used to describe ramp and half-pipe riding, the street style remains by far the most practiced and popular.

In-line skating has never suffered quite the same image or problems. The development of a skate with a single line of wheels, as opposed to the old double-wheeled roller skate, caught the fancy of the public in the late 1980s and early 1990s. Here was a sport soon practiced by both young and old, but it was the younger generation that took the sport to another, more skilled level. Streetstyle contests, as well as the new sport of roller hockey, soon emerged. In addition, skaters followed snowboarders, skateboarders, and BMXers onto ramps and into the half-pipe. Though the action side of the sport (called aggressive in-line skating or *aggro*) isn't as prevalent in the United States as it is in South America, Europe, and Asia, there are still contests, events in the X-Games, and millions of people putting on skates each year.

Looking at the ways in which these sports began, it's still hard to believe that they have come nearly full cycle and are now almost entirely mainstream activities, complete with professional athletes capable of earning millions of dollars through sponsorships and prize monies; product, equipment, and clothing endorsements; and videos and video games. Part of the explanation, however, can be found in the sports culture of the late 1990s and early twenty-first century. More exposure, more money, more television coverage, more people and more tours, make individual action sports the main focus.

There was a time when youngsters' sports heroes were all from the traditional sports. Today, thanks to television and videos, young athletes can admire the likes of skateboarders Rune Glifberg or Tony Hawk, snowboarders Gretchen Bleiler or Shaun White, and BMXers Cory Nastazio, Dave Mirra, or Rick Thorne. These names may not be familiar to everyone, but those who are buying skateboards, snowboards, and the latest model BMX bike sure know who they are—superstars of the same magnitude as a Kobe Bryant, Derek Jeter, or Serena and Venus Williams.

Besides the natural allure of the sport—speed, catching air, and danger—something else is happening to help bring more youngsters to these former alternative sports: an increasing erosion of the attractiveness of team sports. A sobering statistic, compiled recently, shows that of young people starting to play organized team sports at an early age, some 75 percent quit these sports completely by age thirteen. The reasons are complex, but mainly they stem from parents and coaches pushing kids too hard, putting too much emphasis on winning, and pressuring them to work hard so they can earn a college scholarship, win Olympic gold, or even sign a lucrative professional contract someday. Add to these concerns the increasing incidents of violence at youth games, much of it perpetrated by parents and spectators, and the fun is being drained from the game and the sport.

In fact, some young athletes simply prefer individual sports. If you skate-board or ride a BMX bike, you're never second string or sitting on the bench. You won't be told by a coach that you're not good enough to play, and you won't be shunned by teammates because you made a bad play that lost a game. With alternative action sports a rider is on his or her own to practice the kind of discipline that is most appealing, and to be as good as he or she wants to be. Some of today's top riders look back at such experiences when they describe their early attraction to their sport.

"The reason I didn't do team sports was pressure," says Rick Thorne, one of the foremost professional BMX riders on the circuit. "I didn't want pressure from a coach or being beaten down by competition within my own team to be good. I tried soccer and basketball, but it wasn't my style to work with other people. And back when I was a kid, you played team sports or nothing. It just wasn't fun for me. I felt freer when I was on my bike."

Danish-born Rune Glifberg, who was the overall World Cup skateboard-ing champion in 2001, has a similar feeling regarding team and individual sports.

"I always liked individual sports," he related, "with no one telling you how you had to do it. Skateboarding was fun and exciting, fast and danger-ous. A lot of team and traditional sports are repetitive. It's always the same over and over. Hit the ball, make the basket, or score a goal. With skate-boarding and the other individual sports, there are always limitations to be surpassed, a new trick or variation to learn or create, and always progress."

There's yet another reason for the dramatic increase in individual sports. Now that the sports have gone mainstream, to a great degree, parents are ac-tually encouraging their kids to snowboard, skate, and ride. A generation earlier, parents feared these sports and often discouraged their children from playing them, pushing kids toward traditional team sports. No more.

"I see parents of kids between five and ten years old bringing their chil-dren to skate parks and actually coaching them, buying them the boards and wheels they need," Rune Glifberg said. "They see it as a real sport now and that makes it easier on the kids. With the previous generation it was 'What are you doing with that skateboard? Isn't it time to get rid of that?' Parents who used to skate themselves are more supportive. I'm twenty-eight and have a daughter a year and a half old. I know I'll be supportive of anything she wants to do."

Snowboarding, skateboarding, BMX biking, and in-line skating were created much later than traditional sports, but they have quickly taken on a life and character of their own, and they continue to evolve. National exposure via the X-Games, Gravity Games, and other venues are attracting more great athletes who are setting new standards of excellence. However, now that individual sports have entered the mainstream, the other side, that so-called hard-core side that helped create the sports, continues to feature many young athletes who do their thing on the streets and in the parks away from the bright lights and publicity. They are still different, still have an edge to them, an element of danger, and a degree of attitude. And they are just as important to the continued growth of their sports as the mainstream superstars.

Let's take a closer look.

# PART ONE

# SNOWBOARDING

# 1

## A Brief History

Today, the sport of snowboarding is one of the most exciting and daring in the world. Athletes take their snowboards to the top of high mountains, to places accessible only by helicopter, and come flying down untried trails, jumping off ledges and rocks, traversing almost vertical drops, and even taking time to do such tricks as 360–degree turns and a variety of flips. This, however, is not the only form of the sport. Some snowboarders do high-flying, twisting, acrobatic tricks in the half-pipe while others prefer to ride out-of-bounds obstacle courses, jumping and sliding over fallen tree trunks and rocks. The sport has come a long way from the leisurely ride down an open slope, but plenty of people still do that, as well. And it has all happened over the last few decades.

With skiing being such an old and established sport in much of the world, especially in Europe and North America, you might think that snowboarding would have been invented a lot sooner. In point of fact, children living in New England in the early 1920s were building rudimentary boards from barrel staves and riding them sideways down snowy hills. Some point to that as the very crude beginning of the sport.

Snowboarding, surprisingly, has been most influenced by surfing and skateboarding, not skiing. There was, of course, a process of evolution. In 1929, M. J. "Jack" Burchett cut a plank of plywood and secured it to his feet with a length of clothesline and some horse reins, and used that arrangement to slide down a snowy hill. But his and others were isolated projects, backyard boards that never caught on with the general public or were mass-marketed. Much later, in 1963, an eighth-grade student named Tom Sims constructed what he called a "ski board" for a class project, but again there was no effort to market the product. Then, in another two years, along came the Snurfer.

The Snurfer is usually considered the first major breakthrough because it was the first snowboard-like piece of equipment to become commercially available. It was created by Sherman Poppen, who devised the board as a toy for his children. He made the Snurfer by bolting two skis together and putting a rope on the nose that the rider could hold to keep the board more stable. Poppen's wife came up with the name and, before long, the boards were put on the market. They cost only $15 and more than half a million were sold in 1966. Most people considered the boards a toy for their kids.

Jeff Grell is one who remembers the Snurfer well. Born in 1958, he has been part of the snowboarding movement from the beginning and is currently a snowboard World Cup technical delegate and the chief official at certain events. He has helped draw up guidelines for both ski and snowboard instructors and has produced more than 300 events. Not surprisingly, he has played a significant role in snowboarding's history and still climbs on his board whenever he can. Like other early riders, it all started for him with the Snurfer.

"When the Snurfer came on the market," Grell recalls, "my older brother picked one up. We used it on the local hills around Bridgeport, Connecticut, and we got pretty good at it. I'd have to say that, back then, the Snurfer was considered state of the art. We fell a lot, but in fresh snow we could make them turn pretty well. We developed some basic skills, but the Snurfer had no bindings. The rider had to hold on to a rope tether and freedom of movement was hindered by that. Still, it was fun and I used the Snurfer for a number of years."

Soon, other people began developing boards. In the early 1970s, east coast surfer Demitrije Milovich had an idea while sliding on cafeteria trays in the snow of upstate New York. He began to develop snowboards based on short surfboards and skis. He tried rudimentary steel edges, but gave up this idea because he only rode in deep powder. In 1975, the design for his board, called Winterstick, was written up in *Newsweek*, and Winterstick is now considered the first snowboard company.

"The Winterstick was ahead of its time," Jeff Grell said. "You could do things on powdered snow with it that were pretty fantastic for that time. The technique of the board was much better than earlier boards, but it still wasn't good on hard snow."

That problem would soon disappear as snowboard technology began to improve rapidly. Jake Burton Carpenter in Vermont began making boards, one model made from steam-bent wood and another made of fiberglass. Tom Sims at Flight Snowboards also developed boards for harder snow, allowing riders to traverse even difficult terrain.

Then, in 1980, Carpenter and the Winterstick merged to make the new P-Tex board, based on ski technology. Now riders had more versatility and the opportunity to develop consummate skills. The question suddenly became not, What can we use to snowboard? but *Where* can we snowboard?

"In the late 1970s and early 1980s, as more people began riding boards, the ski resorts were still not letting boarders on the same slopes as the skiers," Jeff Grell explained. "The ski industry just didn't know what to make of this new sport. The biggest roadblock then was insurance. Snowboards were classified as snowplay, like a toboggan or a dish. In other words, the insurance industry didn't acknowledge that the rider had control." That meant, in effect, that snowboarding wasn't yet considered a real sport.

But snowboarding wouldn't go away, and eventually there were concessions and progress. The first international snowboard race was held on a mountain called Suicide Six just outside Woodstock, Vermont, in 1982. It was a top-to-bottom race down a steep, icy run called "The Face." It was said that the real object of the race seemed to be survival, because the run was so dangerous. Yet the sport was growing and beginning to attract more participants.

By the early 1980s, however, the situation on the slopes at ski resorts hadn't changed for boarders. Snowboarders still had to find their own places to ride. Jeff Grell remembers doing a great deal of hiking in those days, as did other pioneers of the sport.

"Snowboarders did their riding out of bounds before they could go on the conventional slopes," Grell explained, "because we had to go there to simply ride our boards. Right away, we were in more risk-inherent locations, hiking up avalanche chutes and looking for fresh snow. When I think about some of the places we used to hike it is plain lucky I survived. We started riding in the backcountry before the backcountry became popular, looking for any open-face slope we could access. We used to hike like crazy."

Grell explained how snowboarders in those days were considered loose cannons on the slopes. "People were doing their own things. There were some early competitions, but it seems that the only time snowboarding attracted any attention was when boarders tried to get onto resort slopes and were turned away."

Nevertheless, the pieces were falling into place for a sport that would begin coming into its own just a few short years later. Early slalom contests were held, in which riders raced through a series of gates similar to skiers. The first U. S. Open in snowboarding was held in Snow Valley, Vermont, in 1983, and consisted of a downhill race as well as a slalom run. The first rudimentary half-pipe was dug by hand out of a natural snow bowl in Soda Springs, California, in 1984. All the while, boards were becoming better technically and the sport was attracting more and more participants.

Jeff Grell continued to play a major role as snowboarding burst onto the scene. He recalls riding on the Aspen Highlands in 1983, when the resort opened to snowboarders on a trial basis. "That put me in a situation where I had to negotiate the mountain on a board at a resort that previously hadn't allowed snowboarders," he said. "I found that the bindings I was using had very little ankle support, making it almost impossible to traverse the slope. Without the proper support, the board won't stay flat when you're going from side to side. There was just a toe strap and heel strap holding the feet in place, and the rider had to use the muscles on the top of his foot to put pressure on the board. The stress on those muscles was tremendous.

"That's when I came up with the idea of a high-back binding. The design allowed much of the stress to be taken off the foot. More people were able to learn to use the boards more easily. I think once the concept caught on with the board manufacturers, the sport began to take off."

Finally, some of the big western resorts began opening their slopes to boarders. Grell recalls Aspen was one of the first, as well as Breckenridge, Colorado, another major resort. The smaller resorts waited to see what the larger ones would do, but as of 1985, only thirty-nine of some six hundred resort areas allowed snowboarding. Nevertheless, that situation began changing rapidly as more and more resorts saw the economic feasibility of opening slopes and trails to snowboarders.

"It also didn't hurt that the equipment became increasingly user-friendly during the middle- and late-1980s," Grell said. "Now people who wanted to try snowboarding could rent boots and a board that were pretty easy to use, much more so than the earlier equipment that we all struggled with. More snowboard shops opened and more board manufacturers began springing up. In a nutshell, the sport had become more accessible. At the same time, the resorts also began to offer instruction. I started teaching at the Aspen Highland in 1987—the first teacher there—and many people who wanted to learn began approaching me. At this point, it was pretty apparent that snowboarding was here to stay."

## A Sport Grows and Diversifies

Once the resorts opened up, there was no holding back the sport. Some participants came over from skiing. Others went from skateboards to snowboards during the winter months, while still others saw the sport as pure fun and wanted to try it on their own, with no crossover sports to lean on. Jeff Grell witnessed the growth first hand.

"I've seen a lot of people switch from skiing to snowboarding," he said. "There are some who loved snowboarding so much they said they would never go back. Some just liked the idea of being on one board and cruising around. I still enjoy skiing, as well. It's a different feeling, a different situation. I can go faster on skis, but I can't do a lot of the maneuvering on skis that I can on my snowboard."

Oddly enough, Grell feels that the ski industry changed somewhat because of the snowboarding boom. "Snowcats were the machines used to groom the hills flat," he explained, "but that isn't really the optimum terrain for snowboards. Skiers saw this and now skis are shorter, some of them constructed like snowboards with side cuts that enable skiers to do some of the things snowboarders do. Snowboarding forced the ski industry to adjust itself."

Because of the hazardous-activity law, which makes the snowboarder responsible for his own actions, liability concerns are now largely gone. There was a time when, if there was a dangerous jump on a hill, the ski patrol would shut the hill down. Now, such a risk is acceptable. If someone is injured on the jump, that person is responsible.

The sport began to expand in other ways, too. Half-pipe contests began in the late 1980s. By the 1990s special machines had been designed to cut the snow into almost perfect half-pipes. Today there are even larger machines to create the super-pipes that top professional riders compete in, with perfect transition all the way down so that only the skill of the rider will determine the winner.

"There was a time when we had to hike out of bounds to find the kind of terrain we wanted to ride," Jeff Grell said. "Now places like Mountain High and Big Bear Mountain Resorts in California, for example, have huge terrain parks where snowboarders can go to jump and ride over obstacles. If a rider wants the steepest run, or the deepest powder run, it's there."

Snowboarding is a sport that also attracts girls and women. Circe Wallace, who has been snowboarding since 1984 and began competing in the half-pipe some three or four years later, says women were always a part of the snowboarding scene.

"I was a skateboarder first," says Wallace, who is now retired from professional snowboarding and has become an agent to many action sports stars. "I started learning to snowboard as a recreational thing, but soon decided I loved it and wanted to see how good I could become. More women, however, came over from skiing than skateboarding, but they have been a part of the sport since it was created."

Surprisingly, there were no separate women's divisions in the early half-pipe competitions. The few women who were good enough in the half-pipe competed in the same events as the men. This remained so until the late 1980s, when a separate division was created for women in the sport's various disciplines.

"Now there are more events, more structure, more training facilities," Wallace says. "The infrastructure is in place now and more women continue to come into the sport, which has become more competitive than ever."

Snowboarding became an Olympic demonstration sport in 1994, and four years later it was elevated to a medal sport. That, too, had a tremen-

**Jeff Brushie shows his high-flying style with this huge lean backside Crail.**
**Photo by Shawn Frederick**

dous impact. The beginning of the winter X-Games in 1996 put snowboarding on television; the sport began growing even faster.

"In the early years, when I went out on a hill with my board, people would stop what they were doing, turn their heads and watch," Jeff Grell said. "Nowadays, it's commonplace and nobody turns around. At one time, snowboarding was almost totally a sport for beginners. We'll always have beginners, of course, but now there are more skilled and advanced riders, always looking for ways to improve their performance. You know this when you see people buying a second and third board. They're the ones who will keep at it and who want to improve."

# 2

## Different Ways to Use the Board

It's time to get on the board. Snowboarding is an action sport, the degree of excitement and danger up to the individual boarder and how he or she chooses to ride. Having evolved into a number of separate and distinct disciplines, snowboarding offers a variety of choices, different ways for riders to enjoy their sport. These disciplines vary from basic recreational riding on open, clean slopes, to riding over obstacle-filled terrain. There is also the more traditional racing—slalom and giant slalom, where racers zigzag down a course set off by a series of poles they must go around—that comes directly from longtime skiing competitions. And finally, there are the more spectacular disciplines—competition in the half-pipe; freeriding, which includes boarders who use the entire mountain—anything from a leisurely carve down a moderate slope to riding almost vertical slopes—taking jumps and avoiding obstacles; and freestyle, in which the rider does some astounding tricks, such as the incredible jumps one sees in big-air contests. With so wide a variety of activities, no wonder snowboarding is now a fully accepted major sport.

### Riding for Fun

While snowboarding has become a dynamic and exciting sport, the majority of participants still ride purely for recreation, for fun, and with minimal risks. This is not a difficult sport to learn, though a new rider must be prepared to spend some significant money for clothing and equipment. It is also a good idea for a beginning rider to take a few lessons from an established rider or a professional teacher. This doesn't have to be a long process, just enough to learn the proper stance, balance, and basic ways to control the board.

The board itself is the most important piece of equipment a snowboarder will own. A rule of thumb in any of these sports is to buy the best-quality equipment you can afford. There are currently some very inexpensive snowboards on the market which don't compare with the better boards in durability or performance. If you go to a good ski or snowboard shop, you should be able to learn about the different quality boards and which is right for you. The choice will depend on your skill level, the type of snowboarding you plan to do, and your size. A well-informed clerk is a great source of information.

You will also learn that boards have slightly different styles of construction. In general, boards are now made with a wooden core wrapped in fiberglass and coated in a fiberglass or plastic cap with metal edges. But it is generally believed in the industry today that even the less expensive boards now produced can outperform "signature" series (high end) boards manufactured just five years ago. That's how far the technology has come.

Someone trying the sport for the first few times can rent the equipment they need, then decide about buying their own. A number of factors go into choosing the right board, but the rider's weight is considered the most important when determining the size and type of board to ride. A snowboard is said to act like a leaf spring, so it doesn't really matter how tall a rider is, but how much he or she weighs. When a heavy rider, for example, purchases a board that is too short, the board will have a tendency to "wash out" and perform poorly, especially at higher speeds. A lighter person on a longer board will usually have problems controlling and initiating turns. These are general rules for most snowboarders. The pros and most highly skilled riders will have special board needs and know exactly what they want. Also, the type of discipline a boarder wants to pursue will dictate the kind of board required.

In general, short boards are easier to maneuver and are probably the best choice for a beginner, unless the beginner happens to be very heavy. Short boards are also used by riders doing freestyle tricks in the half-pipe and on slopestyle snowboard courses in parks. The board should come up to the rider's shoulder or chin. Longer boards are used by heavier snowboarders and by advanced riders who jump cliffs and freeride on big mountains, the shape again determined by snow conditions and the style of riding. A longer board can stand up anywhere from the rider's eyes to above the head and is a more solid and stable board to ride at higher speeds as well as when doing more advanced tricks.

The best snowboarders always have a number of boards of varying lengths. Shorter boards are for freestyle tricks such as spinning and flipping, and doing skilled tricks in the half-pipe and in snowboard parks. Shorter boards are also easier to rotate and maneuver, and are used for such street-style tricks as sliding down rails. Top snowboarders may use longer boards for bigger mountain riding with deep powder, and in order to create a more stable platform for landings after big jumps.

Boots should fit snugly when laced and the rider should not feel his heel slipping against the heel of the boot. The foot should not be able to move around in the boot since a snug fit, along with the binding, enables the rider to turn and control the board. There are two kinds of bindings that hold the boot to the board. One is the "step-in" binding, which attaches much more quickly because the rider only has to step in and the bindings snap into place to secure the boot. Step-ins attach the boot to the board either with a toe/heel connection or a side-to-side connection. Most beginners' boards and many rentals feature the easy, step-in bindings for convenience.

The other style is the "strap-in" binding, which takes a little more work and patience, but allows a boarder to perform better. Strap-in bindings are the most popular type of snowboard binding and can be used for both freestyle and freeriding. Most of these bindings have two straps, a toe strap and an ankle strap, as well as a baseplate attached to the board and a high-back piece extending up from the baseplate behind the boot. The straps should be padded and have a ratchet on the ankle strap to help secure the strap snugly to the foot. Some companies also put a ratchet on the toe strap. The highback is what provides the power and leverage for tipping the board on its heelside edge. More power can be applied to the heelside edge with a longer highback.

Bindings also have a swivel adjustment, so riders can place their feet at different angles, and a safety line that clips onto the laces of the front boot. This safety line, or tether, is important. By clipping onto the laces of the front boot, it will prevent the snowboard from sliding away from the rider, should he decide to unbuckle on the middle of the hill. A free-sliding snowboard has been known to cause serious injury to someone directly in its path farther down the hill.

Snowboarders can be comfortable in general-purpose ski clothing. Pants should be warm and waterproof, and riders should always have a good jacket, gloves, and a hat. If riding in the sun, proper sunglasses or a sun shield should be worn, as well, since the snow intensifies the effect of the sun's ultraviolet rays. Beginners, especially, should consider wearing wrist protectors since wrist injuries may commonly occur when riders try to break a fall with their arms and hands. A helmet is an absolute must for all riders, including professionals.

The basics aren't difficult. A new rider must first decide how to be most comfortable on the board. If a rider puts his or her left foot in the front binding and the right in the rear, that is considered the regular way to ride. Placing one's right foot in the front binding is known as "goofy footed." The same term applies in skateboarding, but except for the strange name, it means nothing negative. A rider can select whichever is the most comfortable stance. Whether regular or goofy footed, the skill level that can be achieved will not be affected. The angle of the bindings will become a personal preference, dictated sometimes by the type of riding. For example, a skilled rider may change the angle if he's doing tricks in the half-pipe as opposed to freeriding down a high mountain. Again, an instructor can help beginners. Common freeride settings for beginners have the front foot turned forward 10 to 25 degrees and the rear turned backward up to 5 degrees, somewhat like a duck stance.

Much of snowboarding involves the rider applying the correct pressure on certain areas of the board at just the right time. For example, when going downhill, the rider should apply pressure on the front of the board by shifting his weight toward the front. He won't maintain control if the weight is not centered toward the front of the board. Riders should keep their knees bent, hands low on each side of the body, and always look in the direction they want to go.

Beginning snowboarders will learn quickly how to shift their weight to turn and how to stop the board. They should also know how to fall, just in case falling seems the best option in a particular situation. These basics can be learned very quickly by most people so they can enjoy carving down a slope. Recreational snowboarders often go side to side in large arcs as they come down the hill. Once a boarder can do that and be comfortable on the board, he can consider some of the more advanced disciplines.

## Riding in the Half-Pipe

The half-pipe isn't for the faint of heart. Riding in a pipe takes skill, courage, creativity, and a sense of showmanship. Riders will invariably fall and get hurt, but they must get up, ride again, and persevere. They should also know they are part of a popular and exciting discipline that is highly competitive and can be very rewarding.

Riding the half-pipe has become a popular worldwide discipline for snowboarders. This aspect of the sport derived from skateboarding, which invented riding in the pipe, half-pipe contests, and many of the complex and exciting tricks which crossed over to snowboarding. The half-pipe is exactly as it sounds. It is the shape of a pipe that has been cut in half, so that boarders can ride up one side, catch air as they do a trick, land, and gain speed so they can ride up the other half and do it all again. Skateboarders' half-pipes are made from wood or concrete. With snowboarding, of course, the medium is snow.

Starting in the 1980s, the first "pipes" were simply natural gullies that snowboarders would ride through because it gave them the opportunity to copy skateboarding tricks by riding up one side of the gully and doing a trick while catching air. Later, riders hand-dug trenches which slowly assumed half-pipe shapes. Today, pipes are created by a sophisticated machine called a Pipe Dragon, which can cut a nearly perfect pipe without anyone having to wield a shovel.

Half-pipes have become larger over the years, the height of the walls going from six to nine, and later to twelve feet. Super-pipes, such as the ones used in the 2002 winter Olympics at Salt Lake City, and the 2003 winter X-Games at Aspen, Colorado, have fifteen-foot walls. Now, some are being constructed with walls seventeen feet high and more than 400 feet in length, allowing riders to go faster, catch more air, and do a greater variety of complex tricks.

Let's take a closer look at the half-pipe and the terms used to describe it. The wall is the section of the pipe that slopes up from the flat bottom, and which propels the rider into the air. The transition is the section of a pipe from the flat bottom to the vertical wall. Transitions are measured as the radius of a large imaginary circle. The lip is the upper edge of the pipe where the wall ends, while the deck is the flat area on either side of the pipe where riders can complete a trick or where people can stand and watch.

Some additional terms that describe several of the basics of the tricks performed by half-pipe or super pipe riders, are as follows:

- *Dropping or dropping in.* When a rider starts a run inside the pipe. As he begins going down the side for the first time he is dropping in.
- *Hit.* Each time a rider leaves the lip of the pipe and goes into the air to perform a trick, it is called a hit.
- *Grab.* When a rider does a trick in midair and reaches down momentarily to grab the board. Each grab has its own name, depending on how it is done and with which hand the grab is made. Some basic grab terms are method, stalefish, melancholy, lien, tail, nose, indy, and mute.

  Some examples. The stalefish is a frontside trick where the rear hand grabs the heel edge of the board behind the rear leg and in between the bindings while the rear leg is boned, or straightened. The melancholy refers to a grab where the front hand reaches behind the front leg and grabs the heel edge in between the bindings while the front leg is boned. A nose involves grabbing the front end of the board, and an indy is a grab done with the rear hand grabbing between the bindings on the toe end of the board.
- *Spin, also called rotation.* When a rider goes into the air and spins 360 degrees or more before coming back into the pipe. While spins are measured in degrees, those in the sport often shorten them to simple numbers. The 360-degree spin is called a "3," the 540 a "5," the 720 a "7," and the 900 a "9." The 1080 is still considered so difficult that it usually carries its full name. With riders doing more exciting and daring tricks and spins every day, the 1080 might soon be a "10" with more difficult spins, such as the 1260 or 1440, keeping their full names.

If a 360 represents a complete rotation of body and board, so they are in the same position when the spin started, a 540 is a rotation and a half, a 720 is two complete rotations, a 1080 three complete rotations, and a 1440 four complete spins.

- *Switch, or fakie.* Tricks in which the rider takes off with his opposite foot in front. A "fakie 360" would be a 360-degree spin in which the rider launched with his normally rear foot in the lead.
- *Frontside and backside wall.* The direction in which a rider faces when going up the wall of the pipe. A frontside wall (performed on either side) means the rider is going up on the toeside edge with his back facing down the pipe. Backside is the opposite, with the rider going up on the heelside edge, chest facing down the pipe.
- *Alley-oop.* A very difficult maneuver in which a spin rotates in an uphill direction or back up the pipe. Most spins rotate down the pipe. In the 2002 Olympics, for instance, only one rider attempted big, alley-oop spins.
- *Corked.* Spins that resemble a corkscrew. A corked spin occurs when a rider's body is sideways in the air instead of vertical or level.
- *Inverted.* Any trick in which the rider's head is below his feet while he is in the air.
- *Sketchy.* A trick in which a rider is off balance, not perfect or close to it. A sketchy trick or landing doesn't have to result in a fall, but the term is used when there is enough of an error to deduct points.

Knowing the above descriptions of the physical half-pipe and the terms used by riders will not in and of itself create a star. But anyone interested in riding the half-pipe or even following half-pipe contests and commentary will have a better understanding of what is being done by having this information. Riding the pipe is another thing. It takes a great deal of practice even to approach some of the standard tricks that today are not considered that difficult for good riders.

Jimi Scott is one of the pioneers of half-pipe riding in the snowboarding world. Born in Bellflower, California, in 1968, he began making his mark in 1991 when he won the United States Open Half-pipe Championship. Then in 1993 and '94 he became the Overall International Snowboarding Federation's Half-pipe Champion. Among his many other titles is a gold medal in

This morphed sequence shows veteran snowboard champion Jimi Scott
doing a super tweaked lean air. **Photo by Rob Gracie**

the half-pipe in the 1999 X-Games and, for five straight years (1992–1996)
he was the North American Half-pipe Champion. When it comes to the
pipe, few people have more knowledge than Jimi Scott.

Unlike many of today's young stars, Scott worked his way to the half-pipe
by participating in a slew of related sports. He started surfing when he was
six years old—the beginning of his board-sporting life.

"I surfed for many years professionally," Scott said, "but the competitions eventually turned me off. That's when I found myself skating more, rel-
egating surfing to vacation recreation, a mental release. I roller-skated before
the invention of the in-line skate, then began skateboarding, as well. I was
already participating in vertical roller-skating in a half-pipe and then began
streetstyle skateboarding. It also didn't hurt that I did gymnastics for a while."

Scott became a professional skateboarder in 1984, the same year that the
legendary Tony Hawk turned pro. He followed the professional trail doing
demonstrations, competing in contests, and winning championships. Around

1990, when many skateboard parks were bulldozed due to liability problems, Scott decided to try snowboarding. Because of his background he
picked it up very quickly. Less than two weeks after taking to his board, he
entered the Utah Powder Mountain Winter Games. There were 170 amateurs and 26 pros in the half-pipe event.

"I knew that judges get bored by seeing the same things over and over
again, so I figured, hell, I'll throw balls to the wall, and I won. Having been
a vertical roller skater already used to doing tricks in the air where my feet
were attached, and using the moves I had acquired in skateboarding, snowboarding in the pipe was perfect for me."

In all his years on the circuit, Jimi Scott has some strong opinions about
the half-pipe and advice for those who are thinking about competing in this
form of snowboarding.

"The advanced tricks aren't easy," he said. "Most of them come from
skateboarding and all the snowboarders have done is to embellish them.
However, it takes some daring to do them, as well as discipline and a great
deal of practice. To ride the half-pipe a snowboarder must be in top physical
and mental condition. He also should be instructed on how to do each and
every trick. It's better to be taught or coached. That makes for fewer injuries
and more air awareness. It's difficult for youngsters to learn the tricks correctly just by watching videos. Little things like looking over your shoulder
or under your shoulder will spin you in two different ways, and that's why
coaching is so important."

Scott's advice should be taken—it's dangerous to try difficult tricks in
midair. By having "air awareness," a rider will gain a better sense of controlling his body in the air and how it will react to even the smallest moves sometimes needed to complete tricks successfully.

Jimi Scott has another recommendation for young riders. "Most people
who grow up in the mountains and only snowboard will never get the real
flow of the sport," he believes. "If you come from a surfing or skating background, then you have all the pieces in place. If not, you'll always be missing
something when it comes to the pure style in snowboarding. If you grew up
snowboarding and have never skated you won't know how to grab your
board properly. That's something that comes from skating, where your feet
are not attached and you have to make the grabs to do the tricks success-

fully. There's a flow with riders who have come from the others sports. They stand out, and you can see it immediately. It's like night and day."

As a longtime rider who has looked at his sport through the keen eye of an artist, his point of view is, perhaps, something some young riders will never understand, and some of the contests' judges may not, either.

Of course, as more riders come to snowboarding without a surfing and/or skating background, the judging standards may well change and the flow that Jimi Scott describes could become a thing of the past. All sports evolve; snowboarding is no exception.

Obviously, riding in the half-pipe is not at all like a leisurely carve down a mountainside. It takes more skill, daring, and the ability to take the bumps and bruises of learning. As we will see in the next chapter, the tricks and routines done in the pipe are difficult and complex. But first, let's take a look at more types of snowboarding.

## Freestyle and Freeriding

Freestyle includes a number of styles of snowboarding, giving riders a choice of disciplines to pursue, and the versatility to pursue them. As with the other three sports represented in this book, there is a streetstyle of riding that many snowboarders have enjoyed for years. Wherever there is snow, riders have taken up the challenge of jumping over objects and sliding down others. In very snowy areas, boarders have taken to the streets, jumped their boards over benches, ridden down rails and stairs, and looked for other objects to challenge. The better riders do their tricks while dealing with these natural obstacles in much the same way early snowboarders did when riding out of bounds, the only terrain available to them at that time.

Many snowboard areas now have all-terrain parks set up for this type of freestyle riding, allowing boarders to choose how they want to ride while practicing their skills. In addition, many of the best all-terrain, streetstyle riders can earn a living from making videos, by doing some of their more dynamic tricks, and attracting equipment and clothing sponsors. This type of freestyle remains very popular among young riders who, once again, have taken their style from that of streetstyle skateboarders.

Slopestyle, which also comes under the heading of freestyle, includes judged competitions in which each rider takes his board through a series of jumps, rails, and other obstacles, performing a number of tricks along the way. Many of these riders are highly skilled and do tricks similar to those described for the half-pipe, using spins and grabs, front and backside airs, as well as many flips and other inverted tricks.

Another form of freestyle that has become extremely popular, called freeriding by some, usually involves the boarder coming down an extremely steep route on a high mountain. These are often out-of-bounds runs in backcountry which has to be reached by helicopter or by hiking. At first, riders did such runs for their own enjoyment and expression of freedom. Soon, sponsors began to see freeriding as a way to create spectacular videos with an incredible panoramic backdrop as the rider flew down the mountain at breakneck speeds, jumping off rocks and cliffs, and riding nearly vertical slopes as he made his way to the bottom.

The men and women who chose this kind of riding found it gave them a new sense of freedom, allowing them to pick their own lines down the mountain and do the tricks they wanted to do. Freeriding can be very dangerous, yet riders find that this form of snowboarding gives them a sense of satisfaction they don't get from traditional racing or riding the half-pipe. Freerider Rob DaFoe, explained it this way.

"When you're on a mountain and looking for a cliff to jump, you try to pick the hardest line to go down," DaFoe said. "Anybody can take the easy ones. It's both a poker game and a personal challenge. The best feeling comes from going where no one else wants to go—the idea of competing, finding challenges, and having a personal fight with yourself. And in a sense, it's still somewhat of a dare: *I can do something you can't.*"

Circe Wallace is another who moved from skateboarding to snowboarding. After competing in half-pipe events, she decided to opt for the freedom of the bigger mountains, as well as the opportunity to make some profitable and daring videos, a choice which meant often traveling to remote locations, accessible only by helicopter.

"You can pick your own line when you're in the heli," Wallace said. "You'll be flying over the mountain and decide, *this* is where you want to ride. You have a kind of freedom to be expressive on the mountain, something I've always loved."

However, Wallace and others also know that this kind of snowboarding is not a simple walk in the park. "When you go up in a helicopter in the middle of nowhere and get dropped off on a mountaintop, you're putting your life in the hands of Mother Nature," she said. "It's a really radical, awesome experience. I've had a few close calls with some good-sized sloughs or small avalanches. It's important to be well educated and tuned in to other members of the crew. I want the people with me to have a very good knowledge of the snow, how it appears to be packed, and what it might do as I ride it, so I'll know what to expect. Sometimes snow you think is mellow can be a sleeping giant."

These often wild-and-crazy snowboard runs can last anywhere from thirty seconds to four minutes, depending on the elevations from which the rider begins and the vertical slope of the line. Danger lurks everywhere. There can be an unexpected obstacle, a sudden change of weather, or the ever-present risk of avalanche. Many a top athlete has been claimed in that way, including Craig Kelly, one of the pioneers of snowboard freeriding.

Kelly was one of a group of skiers and snowboarders who were near Revelstoke, British Columbia, Canada, during the last week of January 2003. Having come to ski and snowboard down the Durrand Glacier, a huge avalanche dropped a wall of snow 100 feet wide and 330 feet long on the group. Kelly was one of seven people who lost their lives.

Kelly was not only a multi-time world champion; he was considered the father of the freestyle movement. Jake Carpenter, the renowned snowboard designer and Kelly's main sponsor, said, "He took the sport from competition into freestyle, and the whole industry followed him," Carpenter said. "Then he took it to freeriding, which isn't competition, and the industry following him there. Now, if you pick up a snowboarding magazine, you'll see 90 percent of it devoted to freeriding rather than competition."

There is a point to this story other than to recognize the contributions of Craig Kelly and to mourn his death. Although freeriding can be an extremely dangerous form of snowboarding, more and more riders are taking to the high mountains, out-of-bounds areas, and steep slopes. This is not for the beginner or even the intermediate rider. Only very skillful, advanced snowboarders should try this form of the sport. In addition to having the necessary skills to negotiate these dangerous mountainsides, they must pay attention to weather reports and have a thorough knowledge of weather and snow conditions. Even though an avalanche can surprise even the most experienced rider, a good boarder may avoid potential tragedy by having a thorough knowledge of the snow.

As with other dangerous sports, the occasional tragedy doesn't seem to stop veteran riders or to dissuade new riders from jumping on the bandwagon. Young riders are beginning to push the envelope on the big mountains, just as they are doing with other forms of the sport.

"We're starting to see a technical progression moving over to big-mountain riding," Circe Wallace said, "where people are doing more technical tricks off cliffs. Huge strides are made every year, especially from younger riders. They don't know fear, and this works both to their advantage and to that of the sport. Since more kids are beginning to snowboard earlier and earlier, they're starting out with better fundamental skills."

Rob DaFoe says that he has seen jumps by daring freeriders from a 60-foot cliff of up to 140 feet. These are extremely perilous maneuvers and can easily lead to injury.

"You need the perfect drop and the perfect landing," DaFoe said, "and that's not easy. If you don't jump a certain way from path to landing, you can break your legs every time. Scouting the location and checking out the landing area very carefully are extremely important for a successful jump. You can't go into this area of the sport in a haphazard way. You have to know the rules before you can break them, and know the parameters before you decide to stretch them."

Riders who feel they have acquired the skills to tackle the big mountains should begin by picking an easy line with few difficult obstacles, then gradually work up to more difficult ones that will challenge not only their skill but their courage, as well. Freeriding contests are now being held in the United States, Canada, and Europe, so this daring and dangerous form of the sport is also becoming more mainstream, as the other forms have. There is little doubt that within little more than two decades, snowboarding has gone from a novelty to a charismatic worldwide sport, continuing to grow and attract athletes equipped to take it to the next level.

# 3

## Doing the Tricks

The super-pipe has become the glamour event of snowboarding, both in the eyes of enthusiastic spectators and in the lens of the television camera. This exciting event is highlighted in the winter Olympics every four years, and at the X-Games annually. More young riders are emerging who want to excel in the pipe and emulate today's stars, such as Shaun White. They know the drill. To excel in the half-pipe or super-pipe, they must find ways to embellish most of the existing tricks: go higher, do bigger spins, and choreograph more difficult routines.

The tricks that will be described in this chapter include basic maneuvers being done in the half-pipe and super-pipe today, the majority, as mentioned earlier, having evolved from skateboarding and subsequently copied and embellished by snowboarders over the years. Watching both skateboarders and snowboarders in their respective half-pipes, however, spectators will notice amazing similarities in the tricks being performed. Typical is one called the McTwist.

"I introduced the McTwist to snowboarding," former champion Jimi Scott said. "Mike McGill invented it on the skateboard and Fred Blood had done it four years earlier on roller-skates. When Mike did it on his skateboard, I was already doing it on roller-skates. The McTwist is a 540-degree inverted spin and it takes a lot of practice. That's why I always suggest beginners have some coaching. It will cut down on injuries and give them more air awareness, which is very important."

This sequence of photos depicts the famous frontside McTwist as done by Jeff Brushie. Photo by Shawn Frederick

The McTwist can be done by the rider going up the backside wall. As he comes off the lip he turns his shoulders into the pipe, looking at the tail of his board. Then he twists with his shoulder and grabs the board while he keeps twisting, doing an inverted backflip on the first twist. When he lets go he completes the twist to make it a 540 (one and one-half turns), then lands and continues riding.

Following is a partial list of additional tricks. Remember, they are standard but certainly not all of the ultradifficult tricks done today. These terms, as well as those listed in the previous chapter, will give riders an idea of the possibilities.

- *The 360.* Considered a fairly easy trick to learn. To practice, a rider needs merely to go high in the air. He should approach the jump with good speed and just as he is about to hit it, swing his arms around in front going toward the tail of the board. When he goes off the jump he swings his arms in the opposite direction toward the nose. The body should follow through, making a complete turn in the air before landing. To do a 180, the rider doesn't use as much force and lands facing back toward the jump.

- *The frontside indy.* To do this one, the rider pushes high into the air with his knees. He then grabs the board between his feet with his back hand, does a nose bone (straightening the leg and pointing the board) with his front leg, then lets go and lands.

- *The backside air.* The rider comes up low, goes into the air, then grabs the board between his legs or from the nose, then tweaks, or bends, his rear leg before landing.

- *The method.* As the rider comes to the lip of the pipe or top of a jump, he puts his weight on the backside edge of the board and goes high into the air. He then grabs the board between his two heels with his front hand and arches his back to bring the board around 180 degrees, keeping his chest horizontal and throwing his other hand high in the air as he descends.

**In a morphed sequence, Jimi Scott demonstrates the style needed to complete the method air. Photo by Rob Gracie**

- *The stale fish*. The rider should lean his chest into the inside of the pipe at the same time leaning a bit backwards. As he hits the lip, he pushes up with his thighs, turns his chest toward the board before grabbing it. He should contort his body a bit, turn to the opposite side, and land.
- *The method fakie*. The rider comes up the wall frontside, then extends his feet to the rear while arching his back and twisting his leg as if he were doing an Alley-oop. At this point the rider should straighten out his body and land fakie, that is, with the opposite foot in the lead.

These are a few of the basic tricks being done in the half-pipe. Because they are somewhat difficult to describe, Jimi Scott and other pros always suggest that riders get some coaching when they want to attempt them. Watching videos helps, and there are many available, but only a coach or a veteran rider can point out the little factors that can make a trick successful and minimize danger.

Many riders have invented their own variations on these tricks, and have given them their own slang names. To list all of them here would be virtually impossible. The above list represents only a few. Creative riders will continue to devise their own variations, although most of the basics have already been invented. Jimi Scott, who has been doing tricks like these since 1993, offers a few thoughts on what is happening with the sport today.

"Most everyone thinks that difficult tricks such as 720s and 900s started in 1996, around the same time the X-Games began," Scott said, "but we were doing them in 1993. In 1996 and 1997, when the sport was receiving more mainstream attention, most of the independent magazines were bought out by large publishing companies. They switched focus, concentrating on the hot riders of the moment and forgetting about the guys who really put the sport on the map. In effect, they began to kill the history of the sport.

"The industry today is geared to the product and selling it, to what the athlete can give the industry. For that reason, kids want to get to the top more quickly. When I stopped competing regularly, I was doing 720s and 900s, but kids are now coming in already knowing the 900s and doing 1080s and beyond. My generation discovered snowboarding at a later age, but we had backgrounds in other sports. Today's kids learn the sport much sooner, as early as at age nine or ten, so they enter it at a high level. A lot of them are blowing out earlier, as well.

"They do the same tricks, only bigger. The venues got bigger too, with the advent of the super-pipe. Kids are going higher and doing more while they're in the air, but they have a longer distance to fall, and because of that injuries are up and careers don't last that long. The way the industry looks at it, if a kid breaks his leg, he can't sell equipment, so they dip down and pick the next kid on the list. Kids jockey for position and try to reach the top faster."

Another development in recent years is how quickly girls and women have started to do more difficult tricks in the pipe. "There will always be a gap between men and women," Circe Wallace said, "but I think the gap is closing a bit. I remember watching Shannon Dunn and Kelly Clark (who won gold) at the 2002 winter Olympics, and what they did in the pipe blew my mind. They were doing the same tricks that the men were doing just three or four years ago. Women can never spin and do the same number of rotations as men, but they are getting pretty darn close. If you go back ten years, I think women have progressed much more than men."

Wallace echoes what Jimi Scott said about boarders starting earlier. "The top competitors are definitely younger and it is getting more competitive all the time, so the kids are coming up quick. There's more structure, more events, more training facilities, a natural progression everywhere. I think the athletes have less staying power now because there is always a kid right behind them. To stay at the top, they have to push their physical limitations much more than we did only a few years back."

According to Wallace, the top snowboard competitors are usually men and women between the ages of nineteen and twenty-four. By that age, she feels, athletes have developed enough maturity, physical stamina, and strength, as well as a competitive mindset. "They aren't frightened and won't crack under pressure. They have a better sense of their capabilities."

At the same time she sees some kids as young as fourteen years old doing astonishing tricks. "They have no fear and believe anything is possible. It seems that it's easier for young girls to do these things earlier. Torah Bright at fifteen is doing things that a lot of girls in their twenties are doing. And when a girl can do the same things as some boys at 14 and 15, it's pretty impressive."

Wallace agrees with Jimi Scott that magazines do not present the whole culture and history of this sport. Instead, they concentrate on the young generation, showcasing kids who may not be mature enough to appreciate it. Yet these are the kids who are propelling the sport and the half-pipe tricks to new levels—for example, by landing 1080 spins and going for more—and will continue to do so over the next decade. A perfect example is Joe Eddy, a 17-year-old who landed an incredible 1260 at the 2003 winter X-Games.

Some of the tricks used in the half-pipe can also be used in both freestyle and freeriding. We've already mentioned slopestyle contests, where riders do tricks, many of them spectacular, over a series of jumps. Even freeriders, especially when they are being filmed for a video as they come down a steep line of descent will do a few tricks when taking jumps and going over hills. Many of these riders have also spent time in the half-pipe, so they already have the training and the knowledge to do the same kind of spins, twists, and grabs they did in the pipe.

Airborne tricks have become a major part of snowboarding and the aspect of the sport that has drawn the most attention. While some people are undoubtedly satisfied merely to hit the slopes for a leisurely day of carving down a mountain, many young people coming into the sport will sooner or later look to emulate the tricks being done by the superstars who compete at the Olympics, in the X-Games, and are featured in scores of magazines and videos.

Now let's look at the way contests are judged and how they have become a major part of mainstream sports.

# 4

## The Importance of Contests

If you want to locate a starting point for the alternative sports movement, you need only to look back at the skateboarding culture that arose in southern California in the 1980s, when young athletes began taking to their boards and strapping on their in-line skates. Although these early riders were often looked upon as rebels and, sometimes, pests, they began developing amazing skills on their boards and skates. Adults often criticized their clothes, hairstyles, tastes in music, and whatever else didn't appear "normal," but these things were part of their culture, part of a lifestyle they adopted along with their riding.

This group of young athletes, which soon became known as the MTV Generation and Generation X, continued to advance in skill and recruit new riders for their sports. By the mid-1990s, most of the alternative sports were growing in popularity. By the time snowboarding became an Olympic demonstration sport in 1994—its first real move into the mainstream—each sport had its magazines and a cult of followers. What they still needed was a major, national stage. Along came the ESPN X-Games.

Ron Semiao, program director for ESPN2, came up with the idea for the X-Games in 1993. He decided he wanted to showcase sports that "have a whole culture attached to them, a specific attitude and a group of people who live and die for that sport."

The board sports, BMX biking, and in-line skating were all perfect for the new event. Because of the difficulty each had in finding acceptance, they were considered sports with an attitude, which is what Semiao was looking for. The summer X-Games began in 1995 and the winter games two years later. Not only did the X-Games bring these sports to a wider audience via television, they also created opportunities for athletes and sponsors who hadn't been there before. More videos were produced, advertising became more widespread, and more corporations decided to commit funds for sponsoring alternative sports. The X-Games have played a large role in bringing these sports into the mainstream, helping the entire industry to grow, not only from an athletic standpoint, but by encouraging more companies to manufacture equipment and clothing for athletes. By 1998, the summer X-Games at San Diego drew an estimated 250,000 fans in addition to a television audience estimated to be about 74 million. There is little doubt that the X-Games were here to stay.

From the start, snowboarding was one of the showcase events of the winter X-Games. The contest in the super-pipe is a highlight for fans everywhere, and all the top riders compete for the gold. The same excitement exists in the winter Olympics, where winning athletes can say they are not only the best, but can, with any luck, turn their gold into dollars.

## How Are the Contests Judged?

Most snowboarding contests are judged in very similar ways. Athletes will drop into the pipe and hope to do a series of their best tricks as they ride up one side, then the other side, of the pipe, as part of a prepared routine.

"You try to choreograph your runs to your own music," veteran Jimi Scott explained. "And you try to do certain tricks in special parts of the pipe because the judges can see you better there. Some riders will plan and practice a certain routine and then do it over and over again. But the judges look for change in the routine from one run to the next, and the top riders do that. Some riders feel they have perfected only a number of tricks and they, too, will do the same run over and over. In the end, that becomes stale. Champions change and there are only a handful of them who can do any given trick in any situation. They are the best."

All contests are judged similarly. After some preliminary runs, those who make the cut face the final runs. Offered here is a description of how the half-pipe competition was judged in the 2002 winter Olympics, where five judges each score a specific aspect of the performance. One scores *straight airs,* one *rotations,* one *amplitude,* and the two others both score *overall impression,* which is worth double points, making the highest total for a run fifty points. The categories are evaluated as follows:

1.  *Straight airs.* The straight air judge looks mainly for style. This means that the rider must go high in the air and grab the board solidly, holding the grab or even "tweaking" (bending a leg) or "boning" it out (straightening or extending a leg) at the peak of the trick, then re-entering the pipe smoothly. The straight air judge will look at every trick in a rider's performance up to a 360-degree spin. A typical straight air occurs when a rider goes into the air, grabs the snowboard, and turns 180 degrees to reenter the pipe in the same direction as the takeoff.

2.  *Rotations.* The rotations judge rates any trick with a spin over 360 degrees. This includes, of course, 540s, 720s, 900s, and the spectacular 1080s. The rotations judge watches for degree of difficulty, as well as style and smoothness. Spins with a grab are typically scored higher than spins without a grab.

3.  *Amplitude.* Amplitude is how high the rider gets out of the pipe and into the air. Gold medal winners can soar as high as fifteen feet above the coping. In most runs, the very first hit at the top of a run is the trick with the most amplitude because the rider has a long run-in to gather speed. The amplitude judge looks also for the riders who can maintain the most height throughout the run.

4.  *Overall impression.* The two overall impression judges consider an entire run, taking into account such things as whether the rider performed difficult tricks back-to-back or if one trick flowed smoothly into the next. They also look for variety: whether the run had a mixture of straight airs, spins, and inverted maneuvers, and if the rider maintained both smoothness and style throughout the run.

As a rule, riders performing difficult tricks at the beginning of the run are taking more risk than if they save them for the end. If a rider falls while try-

**This sequential shot captures Rob DaFoe demonstrating a frontside cowboy 540.** Photo by Shawn Frederick

ing a difficult trick at the outset, his entire run is ruined. It's too difficult to get speed up again after a fall. However, judges will reward riders who take risks early in their runs, as well as those who perform combinations of difficult tricks, one after the next. As Jimi Scott said, it's the champions who take the risks and add variety.

The 2003 winter X-Games, which took place in Aspen, showed probably better than anything how far snowboarding in the super-pipe had come. Competitors in both the men's and women's divisions put on a spectacular show that had fans gasping in awe. The acrobatic and skill level was simply amazing and everyone got a glimpse of the future in the form of Shaun White.

White was just sixteen years old at the time of the games. Only a year earlier he had said, flat out, "Gotta come back next year and win this piece." But that wouldn't be easy. To illustrate just how many top competitors there are now, the three Olympic medalists from the 2002 winter games—Ross Powers, J. J. Thomas, and Danny Kass—hadn't secured a place in the finals after completing the first qualifying runs, the first step taken in paring the field down to ten finalists. All three would make it on their second run and the ten elite riders prepared themselves to go for the gold.

The final runs produced some extraordinary tricks that only the best riders in the world dare even try. For example, seventeen-year-old Joe Eddy actually landed a 1260, going the very difficult 1080 one better. Marku Koski, who would finish third, was the first rider to stomp (a good landing) the 1080 and the only one throwing switch methods (doing the trick backwards), switch alley-oop (rotating in an uphill direction) indys, and the elusive switch alley-oop backside rodeo.

Danny Kass, who finished second, unleashed a triple-poke 720 into an inverted cab (a trick that begins backward, with the rider landing forward) 1080 mellon (a grab of the heel of the board while doing the difficult 1080 rotation), which one judge called the most stylish combination of the day. Someone described his cab 1080 mellon as "a stunning combination of madness and precision."

As good as Koski and Kass were, Shaun White was even better. Appearing with a red cowboy bandana wrapped around his face, White proceeded to link together an amazing run of tricks. He started with a massive McTwist into an incredibly huge and smooth frontside 900. After hitting it perfectly, he blended in big leins (the front hand grabbing the heel edge as the body leans out over the nose), backside airs and a set-up 720, and a gold-medal-winning run.

"I don't know," White said, "the sun came out and I got all stoked. I just wanted to have some fun and it turned out sick." Asked about his incredibly smooth 900, White added, "I try to do 1080s all the time and when I learned those, it made 9s super-easy."

Perhaps White's victory was best summed up by Todd Richards, who had won the gold medal in the 2000 games, but was out of this one with an injury.

"I wish I were sixteen and that good," Richards said of White.

On the women's side, the excitement and the skill was equally evident. The gold medal was won by Gretchen Bleiler, 21, who was also the 2002 Triple Crown champion, in one of the great performances in X-Games history. To win, Bleiler had to unseat the defending champion, Kelly Clark, 19, and fend off Hannah Teter, 16, who finished third.

Clark's run in the final featured an enormous air at the top, a huge frontside 540, followed by a corked backside 540 with a tail grab; then she stomped a frontside 720 and took the lead. "It meant a lot to me that I hit that run," she said. "I've been having some trouble lately, and I needed to bring my confidence back up."

It wasn't over, by any means. Teter's final run included a perfect 900 in a run that showed some of the biggest air and style of the competition. Remember, there was a time when women weren't close to men in rotations. A sixteen-year-old had now landed a perfect 900. But finally it was up to Bleiler, who had fallen during her first qualifying run and had to come back strong. She said she was pumped up by the outstanding final run of her good friend and riding partner, Kelly Clark.

"I was so stoked to see Kelly come out with a sick run like that," she said. Then Bleiler went to work and topped her friend. She began by stomping a huge crippler (a frontside inverted 540) at the top of the pipe and followed that with smooth back-to-back backside 540s and a frontside 540. Her performance brought her the gold medal. Yet even with her incredible success, she, like the other men and women, saw more difficult tricks ahead.

"The level is huge now," Bleiler said. "It's all inverts, amp, and spins now. I'm working on nailing that crippler 7 and a 900 next time around."

The 2002 X-Games was a resounding success and once again saw snow-boarding reaching yet a higher level. Circe Wallace had predicted this kind of performance when she said the women were closing the gap with the men.

"Kids are riding year-round now," she said, "learning at camps, watching the pros and talking to them. Some of the best go to Mount Hood and train with veteran pros and have their own coaches."

Jimi Scott's concern is that kids will see the success of a Shaun White and push too hard to reach that same degree of achievement. "I see many more severe injuries because the level of riding is so high," he said. "Kids don't always understand the importance of hiring a trainer and doing the proper rehabilitation. While the tricks are bigger, the number of injuries is increasing, as well."

But injuries have never stopped these incredible alternative sports athletes. To many of them, a broken ankle is like a sprained finger to the average person. They heal as quickly as they can and get right back out there, trying even more difficult tricks than before their injury. So the superpipe riders will continue to take snowboarding to new and higher levels in their pursuit of perfection . . . and championships.

# 5

# A Growing Sport for Everyone

Don't ever tell a snowboarder that he is participating in a minor sport. To an avid rider, being on the board is everything, the best thing he can do. Recent polls prove that the sport is enjoying unprecedented growth. In fact, snowboarding has become a sport for everyone in a relatively short period of time. A quick look at the numbers will bear that out. A National Sporting Goods Association (NSGA) survey of all sports showed the percentage of change in the number of participants in two age groups between 1991 and 2001. Of all the sports surveyed, snowboarding showed the largest growth.

In the 7-to-17-year-old age group, snowboarding showed a 238.8 percent increase in participation during that ten-year period. (The second largest increase came in the sport we are going to discuss next, skateboarding, which increased some 163.1 percent.) Broken down even further, snowboarding participation increased 263.0 percent among those ages 7 to 11, while the 12-17 age group increased 186.5 percent. As our experts said, the kids are starting out a lot younger now.

Another NSGA survey showed the percentage of increase among participants age 7 and up from 1996 to 2001. This time, skateboarding ranked first with a 106.3 percent increase, while snowboarding was next at 72.4 percent. The third largest increase came in backpack/wilderness camping, much lower at 26.5 percent, while golf was fourth at 15.4 percent. These figures make it apparent that snowboarding continues to grow and become increasingly popular.

Such growth doesn't mean that everyone who snowboards will become a star in the half-pipe or try to reach the X-Games and compete in the super-pipe. Some people will be content to travel to a resort during their vacation and strap a snowboard on only a few times a year. Others will fall in love with the sport and the atmosphere that surrounds it, enjoying the brisk winter air and the sense of freedom that comes with a ride down a mountainside.

Then there are those who will become part of the snowboarding culture. They may be former surfers, skateboarders, or skiers. In some cases, they may indeed start out as snowboarders because of the increasingly high visibility the sport now receives. In any case, these are the riders who may pick one of the more dangerous or exciting disciplines. Those in cities with sufficient winter snowfall can take to the streets and emulate skateboarders who jump obstacles, slide down rails, and ride over benches. Some may prefer the new, all-terrain parks many resorts are building, which combine the street-style with out-of-bounds riding, one of the sport's several freestyle disciplines.

Those with an array of skills and a competitive nature may opt to learn the difficult tricks in the half-pipe, with an eye toward Olympic or X-Games gold, while others may be intrigued by the prospect of riding down high, steep mountains over untried terrain, a freeriding experience that can be as dangerous as it is fulfilling.

Thanks to the sport's greater visibility, more snowboarders have the opportunity to become professionals. Top riders are now able to earn a very comfortable living though prize money, sponsors, videos, and demonstrations. Former competitors have also remained in the sport in other capacities. Circe Wallace has become an agent, representing athletes in all the alternative sports. Jeff Grell is a snowboard World Cup technical delegate, the chief official at certain events, as well as a judge and instructor. Jimi Scott coaches two snowboarding teams, including one at the University of Colorado, and is the director of terrain park operations at Eldora Mountain Resorts.

"Coaching gives me the most excitement now," he says. "When I teach and a kid gets it, it's a real rush."

**Ross Peterson shows how the switch boardslide is done.** Photo by Rob Gracie

With all this activity, the arrow appears to be pointing up for the future of snowboarding. The numbers are increasing and the competitive athletes are doing bigger and better things. In addition, the sport continues to generate more fans and more acceptance from corporate America. There's little doubt that snowboarding is now in the mainstream of worldwide sports.

"In the next ten years, I think, the sport will become even more mainstream," Jeff Grell said. "New people continue to get up on snowboards, though it's leveling off a bit from the explosion of the early 1990s. But there are more opportunities now, the caliber of the athletes is higher and there are certainly better facilities and equipment. It's a sport I'll continue to pursue actively as long as I'm fit enough to do it. It's part of me now. If I didn't snowboard for two years, I know I could still get up on that board and it would immediately seem as if it were yesterday."

For snowboarding, the yesterdays will always be there and the tomorrows continue to come.

# PART TWO

# SKATEBOARDING

# 6

## A Brief History

In many ways, skateboarding is the granddaddy of all the alternative sports, the discipline from which the others evolved. Some may have come first, but skateboarding was the first to have the rebel or outlaw image, its own subculture where kids dressed and spoke differently and closed ranks in an us-against-them mentality. Its history dictated that. It's probably safe to say that no other activity has had quite the same overall effect in creating a sports counterculture and influencing several generations of youngsters.

Skateboarding is a sport with a history full of ups and downs, high and lows—the lows sometimes threatening to relegate the sport to back alleys and other out-of-the-way places. No one wanted skaters rolling through their streets, sidewalks, parking lots, and local parks, but kids wouldn't let their sport die. Called outlaws and rebels, and sometimes lawbreakers, the early generation of skateboarders had their own clothes, their own music, defiant symbols on their boards, and their own ways of doing things. They refused to be told, NO YOU CAN'T!

Today, skateboarding is a huge sport with more than ten million participants, though it still retains its own individual aura that tells skaters that they still control their sport. It has done this while becoming commercially successful, and is now a mainstream sport, one of whose longtime superstars, Tony Hawk, is arguably more popular and recognizable among the younger generation than Kobe Bryant or Alex Rodriguez, two of the biggest names in basketball and baseball. In addition, today's skateboarding stars are doing some amazing tricks in the half-pipe—spins, flips and big airs—while ordinary kids still take to the streets and show incredible skill and dexterity in jumping over obstacles and riding down rails. How did such a relatively simple sport, using a board and some wheels, become so attractive to so many athletes of all ages, and become a huge industry at the same time?

It's necessary to look back to the early years of the twentieth century to find the first crude skateboard-like devices. These vehicles, which resembled scooters but without the long handle, were made simply by attaching roller-skate wheels to a two-by-four. Kids would often mount part of an old milk crate to the boards, nailing it vertically to the front, providing the board with handles so the rider would have some control. Experimentation with basic design began during the first half of the century, with various kinds of boards and wheels tinkered with to give people a different kind of ride. Steel roller-skates provided the first wheels. Skates were often dismantled and their wheels hammered onto different boards and planks of wood.

By the 1950s, trucks (the name for the piece that holds the wheels on the board) were designed which allowed riders to maneuver better on their boards. At the same time that these developments were taking place in skating, the sport of surfing began gaining in popularity. It wouldn't be long before people began to realize that the two sports were closely related. Surfing in the ocean and skateboarding down the boardwalk or street had many similarities. The feeling of the ride wasn't all that different. It was in 1959 that the first commercial board, the Roller Derby Skateboard, appeared on the market and young athletes began to buy it in increasing numbers.

The 1960s saw skateboarding beginning to find a growing following among surfers, especially in California. Larry Stevenson, who published the *Surf Guide*, began to promote skateboarding and soon formed a company called Makaha, which designed the first professional boards. In 1963 he formed a team of skateboarders to promote his product. More firsts followed. The first skateboarding contest was held at the Pier Avenue Junior School in Hermosa, California, in 1963, and a year later a surfing legend named Hobie Alter teamed up with Vita Pakt juice company to produce Hobie Skateboards.

By that time skaters were starting to ride the streets and sidewalks of their communities, while others sought out banks and ditches. Some rode in empty swimming pools, using the slopes from the deep end to the shallow end— and, in some cases, the sloping walls—to ride out of the pool and catch air. In three years, from 1962 to 1965, some fifty million skateboards were sold—an enormous number—and by 1965 there were international contests, a movie called *Skater Dater*, a magazine devoted to the sport, *The Skateboarder Quarterly*, and cross-country trips by teams of skaters intent on demonstrating the sport to potential new riders. Then, suddenly, the sport began the roller-coaster ride that is now part of its history and lore.

In a nutshell, skateboarding almost died in the fall of 1965. Part of the problem was the product. The boards weren't good enough to keep up with the increasing skills of the riders. Companies maintained too much inventory and, as soon as the boards stopped selling, great amounts of money were lost. At the same time, people were becoming fed up with kids skating on the streets and sidewalks, often in what was considered a reckless manner. Riders often fell, and the few fatalities received an overblown amount of publicity. Because of safety concerns, the sport was banned in most areas of many cities, and those who loved the sport felt they had nowhere left to skate.

Dave Duncan, born in San Diego in 1962, started skateboarding around the age of twelve and he has played a major role in the industry ever since. He became a professional in 1987, and a year later he got involved with the National Skateboard Association, organizing its professional events nationwide. In fact, Duncan has been a part of almost every aspect of the sport, working with World Cup organizers, judging events, announcing, building ramps, and designing skateboard parks. He knows as much about skateboarding as anyone.

"My brother had an old, steel-wheeled skateboard in the 1960s and began riding on the driveways and sidewalks," Duncan recalls. "I would see kids on these boards cruising down the sidewalks, not doing many tricks, trying hard to make turns. The boards were not very maneuverable. Kids fell so often that they began calling the boards "bunbusters," after the Jan and Dean song, 'Bust Your Buns.' But the surfers loved skateboards. They would ride the waves in the afternoon and ride the streets on skateboards."

Unlike some skateboarders, Dave Duncan was an all-around athlete as a kid and played all the team sports. But once he began to skate, skating and surfing became his two favorite sports. He began also to ski and snowboard, and soon left traditional team sports entirely.

"I found something so gratifying, it gave me a tremendous amount of satisfaction. There was a sense of fulfillment when you accomplished something new on the board. You would watch a guy do a trick and then see if you could do it. When you did, it took you to another level, and you got a pat on the back from your peers. The mindset wasn't the same as in team sports, where you play to win. Here, you play around with this toy to see what you can do and it really gives you an adrenaline rush. If you fell, you knew you would get scraped up, and on days you didn't get hurt, you felt pretty good.

"Skateboarding brought together an interesting group of people. I've found skaters to be free-thinking individuals who really respect each other. It's a sport in which different types of people can be the best of friends merely because they skate. There's no race or economic prejudice in skateboarding. All skaters have one thing in common, their boards and their skills, and that's enough."

Early on, however, Duncan noticed that people who didn't skate had certain perceptions about those who did. "Skateboard kids were looked down upon because people saw no future in it. No one was making money in those early days and it was assumed that skateboarders wouldn't amount to anything. Because we skated so much of the time, people felt we didn't care about anything else, including school. At the same time, because we were looked down upon by so many people, our attitude became, *Just leave me alone to enjoy my world.*"

The ups and downs of the sport didn't make acceptance any easier. During one of the "downs" in the late 1960s and early 1970s, however, steel wheels were replaced by wheels made of clay—a major improvement. "Clay wheels lasted longer, had more grip, and riders could do slides with them," Dave Duncan explained. "They were wider and didn't vibrate as much. Someone doing a lot of riding would have to replace them every week or two. The ball bearings became loose and would sometimes fall apart while we were riding on them."

According to Duncan, skaters at the time built their own boards, taking the trucks and wheels from commercial boards and using three-quarter-inch plywood for the board. Sometimes, they would make a new board almost every day. "Since many of the riders were surfers, as well, they drew pictures of surfers on their skateboard and put resin over the drawings so that they would look like commercial boards. Or they would cut pictures of surfers from magazines and use them on the boards.

"I remember surfing teams also assembling skate teams," Duncan continued. "The first skateboard tricks emulated surfing. Riders would do handstands on their boards, as well as maneuvers such as tic-tacs, a way to gain speed without pushing. A tic-tac is done by lifting the nose and putting it down on your right, then lifting it again and putting it back down on your left. Doing this rapidly will pump the board in a forward direction. Riders also challenged each other on how many 360s each could spin. They would spin like ice skaters and that took talent. Everything then was pretty much done on a flat surface."

By the early 1970s, skateboarding was still almost an underground sport, rarely seen outside of certain areas on the California coast. Though it would take another few years for the sport to return to popularity, something happened in 1970 that would change the face of skateboarding forever. A man named Frank Nasworthy visited a friend at a plastics factory in Virginia where urethane wheels were made for a chain of roller rinks. When Nasworthy realized that urethane wheels would fit on his Hobie Skateboard and tried it out, he decided to develop a skateboard wheel made of urethane. At first, promoting the product in the San Diego area, he didn't have much success. But slowly, word began to spread throughout California about the new product and more skaters began buying it.

"Urethane wheels opened up a new world for skaters," says Duncan. "They had more grip. You could torque a turn hard, and go very smoothly on them. They allowed you to ride on sand and other rough surfaces, and you could skate for weeks at a time without changing them. In addition, the urethane wheels were part of a sealed system so that the bearings wouldn't fall apart. They made the boards complete."

## Second Boom

The advent of urethane wheels helped make possible skateboarding's second boom period, in 1973 and 1974. New companies sprung up to manufacture boards, trucks, and wheels. The sealed, precision bearings which Dave Duncan described became available in 1975, further stabilizing boards. New publications, such as *Skateboarder Magazine*, ran photos showing kids riding in pools, making their own ramps, and doing new and more difficult tricks. In 1976, the first outdoor skate park was built in Florida, and in a short time hundreds of similar parks were springing up all over. Park designers began creating areas similar to empty swimming pools and drainage ditches in the parks, an innovation which allowed the sport to become more vertical, with riders flying out of the "pools" and "ditches" in the parks. The older slalom style, which emulated ski racing through gates, quickly lost popularity.

Boards began changing around this time, as well. They became wider, going from six to seven inches in width to more than nine. This widening gave riders more stability on vertical surfaces. In 1978, Alan Gelfand invented the ollie, a move that allowed a rider to go in the air without the board falling from his feet. This maneuver allowed skateboarders to push many new tricks and variations to the limit, such as jumping over and off objects and turning in the air without losing the board. At the same time, the first real stars of the sport began to emerge.

"Tony Alva was, in my mind, the Tony Hawk of the 1970s," Dave Duncan said. "He became a media darling, doing some amazing aerial maneuvers, and he was regarded by the younger generation in the same way Tony Hawk would be ten years later. In fact, Tony Alva showed me that if you were good enough to ride the parks you would have a lot more fun. It made me want to become a better rider and I know many others thought so too.

"Jay Adams was another top rider during that period. If Alva is considered the grandfather of the sport, Adams would be his brother. They had two distinctly different styles. Tony was a real pro while Jay was wild and exciting."

It was around this time that a new kind of skateboarding culture—streetstyle—was born. Streetstyle developed as riders started using aerial moves on flat land. At the same time, the riders associated themselves with punk rock and new wave music, and more macabre images, such as skulls, began appearing on the boards, all of which would contribute to the skaters' rebel or outlaw image.

When liability insurance began to become a major concern at the skateparks, insurance premiums rose so high that park owners couldn't afford to pay them. The result was that parks began disappearing around 1980, many of them bulldozed out of existence.

"By 1982, almost all the parks were gone and the sport slowed down again," Dave Duncan remembers. "Once more it was only the hardcore skaters who kept at it. Again, boom turned into bust. The economic recession of 1983 hit the industry hard, and kids were forced to ride the streets. That's when the punk image really began to appear. If kids weren't in their own backyards, they were on the sidewalks, mixing with pedestrians, or on the streets, mixing with traffic. They would be given tickets for riding the streets or building ramps. There was almost no place they could ride. Here they had found something they considered really great and they had no place where they could ride and have fun."

"Many skaters also had a new look. They cut their hair real short, as opposed to the long hair of the so-called hippies, and became somewhat outlaws," Dave Duncan said.

Nevertheless, a few contests continued to be held. While no one made much fuss when a young Tony Hawk won his first contest at the Del Mar Skate Ranch in 1982, a time when riders had few outlets, Hawk and others would soon have a much bigger stage on which to shine. By 1984 vert riding (catching air off ramps and hills) and streetstyle skating (riding over, on, and around obstacles such as benches and rails) became extremely popular, and more riders began to compete in the half-pipe.

"Tony Hawk came of age during the 1980s," Dave Duncan said. "He and Christian Hosoi dominated the sport. Christian had the most style. He loved the big vert ramps and flew higher than Tony. He always did the biggest aerials and had the most stylish power moves. Tony possessed more technical wizardry. He did big tricks no one else in the world could do, and it seemed as if he showed up at every competition with a new one. He was always one step ahead of everyone. Another great rider during the 1980s was Mark Anthony, known as "Gator." He was an all-terrain rider who could do everything, and all three of these guys hung out together often."

When another economic recession in the early 1990s slowed the progress of the sport, Dave Duncan said, many older skaters abandoned it and younger athletes took over, once again directing skateboarding away from the popular half-pipe and back into the streets. Pool skating, a tradition since the beginning, completely died out and 90 percent of young skaters could be found riding streets and sidewalks.

This was a time, Duncan recalled, "when a lot of the young kids in baggy pants did technical tricks on the streets—very technical and often slow maneuvers. They earned the respect of their peers because the tricks were especially difficult. Commercially, however, endorsements were few, and not even Tony Hawk had a board model. He went into retirement for a few years."

Nevertheless, skateboarding—the sport that wouldn't die—reemerged in the mid-1990s. In 1993, the National Skateboarding Association became World Cup Skateboarding and organized more competitions in the United States as well as in Australia, Brazil, Canada, and across Europe. Two years later, when the X-Games were held for the first time, skateboarding attracted legitimate television exposure. This was mainstream exposure at the professional level.

"The advent of the internet didn't hurt, either," said Dave Duncan. "Magazines went on-line, and skaters could watch videos and exchange photos. Video games began to feature skateboarding. Many of these games were very realistic and allowed kids to not only play the game, but to see how various tricks were done."

With the X-Games and, later, the Gravity Games, more prize money was offered and more corporations sponsored riders who, in turn, endorsed their boards and clothing, as well as such items as soft drinks and sunglasses. The top pros were able to make livable incomes from skateboarding, some earning rather large amounts. The final element, one which pretty much ensured that skateboarding would not die again, then fell into place: Dave Duncan and others led a fight to change liability laws. As of 1997, skateboarding was declared a hazardous activity, which freed city skateboard parks of liability. Now a rider, or his or her family, cannot file suit, claiming, for example, a ramp was too steep. Skaters proceed at their own risk. The new legislation was a boon to parks and, according to Duncan, during the past five years more than a thousand skate parks have been constructed around the country.

"Exposure today is at hyperspeed," Duncan said. "We've been playing catch-up for the last twenty years. Now, we're finally getting the exposure we should have had all along. There's been a huge boom and any kid who wants to learn to skate can now do it."

It was a long, hard battle, won perhaps only because hard-core riders refused to quit. They kept riding when people said they couldn't or shouldn't. They kept riding when there was no official place to ride. And they kept riding when they were called outlaws or rebels. They loved their sport and, eventually, convinced others to try it. Because of them, the granddaddy of all board sports became a kid again.

# 7

# Skating in Style—All the Basics

Skateboarding is rarely a leisurely activity. On the contrary, it's often an out-front, in-your-face sport, where the boldest rider is the one who excels, and the street riders still rule. Sure, it's possible to use a skateboard as a means of transportation, to push off and skate from point A to point B just to get somewhere a little faster. That, however, may be how some riders begin, and better riders do as an afterthought. Most, however, want to test their boards and their skills each time they go out to skate. There probably isn't a skateboarder around who hasn't had the urge to push a little harder and go a little higher. They may start with simple tricks, and may progress to more technical and difficult maneuvers. And if they're really daring, they'll go vertical, begin catching air, and flying as high as they can.

As with the other board and riding sports, there are always choices to be made. Some skateboarders specialize in one style, such as the half-pipe, while others may prefer streetstyle, jumping over obstacles and grinding, or sliding, down rails. Because of changing attitudes and rules, styles have come and gone, merged and changed. Briefly, let's take a quick look at three old styles of skateboarding, and then the three styles that are most popular today.

## The Old Styles

- *Pools.* Pool riding began in drained swimming pools with a bottom that had transitions—in other words, sloped sides and no L-shape walls. Pool style can also mean riding in a manmade concrete bowl that is much like a swimming pool. Pool riding was part of the early skateboarding scene and was often featured when the first skateboard parks were built, as the parks contained concrete replicas of drained pools. There are very few riders who only do pools today, but vert riders often like to jump from a facsimile of a pool in a skatepark and catch some air.

- *Banks.* Early skaters often looked for natural banks on which to ride, but they weren't always easy to find. A bank is a slope with no transitions, which are curved surfaces used to pick up speed, as in the half-pipe. It is generally steep enough to ride up once and catch enough air for one trick. Riders cannot go back and forth as in the half-pipe or even in a swimming pool. Again, kids who find a bank will ride it, but there are no specialty bank riders today.

- *Flatland or freestyle.* Flatland riding was another popular form of skateboarding in the late 1970s. Often more about style than tricks, it was once compared to figure skating in so far as the riders strung together combinations of fairly simple maneuvers, performed in a flowing, stylish manner. Riders might do handstands, sometimes using two boards, as well as jumps, turns, and spins. It's a style that is probably too slow and confining for today's riders, who prefer to attain more speed and to catch air.

## The Current Styles

- *Street.* Streetstyle skating has been around in one form or another since the sport began, and it is by far the most popular form today. In effect, it's a no-holds-barred style, in which any natural object is fair game for the rider to challenge, including tricks done off stairs, railings, benches, low walls, curbs, and launch ramps—anything that can be jumped or

**Freeriding snowboarder Andy Dunham goes airborne as he does an indy cliff drop during a mountain run.** *Photo by Shawn Frederick*

**Jeff Brushie grabs his board while flying through the backside Crail air maneuver.** *Photo by Shawn Frederick*

**Josh Schoenfeld demonstrates the technique used to do the layback carve.** *Photo by Shawn Frederick*

**Josh Schoenfeld doing a picturesque powder carve, something even new snowboarders can quickly learn.** *Photo by Shawn Frederick*

# SKATEBOARDING

**Skateboarder Lincoln Ueada shows a portion of the technique needed to do the frontside finger flip.** *Photo by Shawn Frederick*

**Copenhagen-born champion Rune Glifberg completing a frontside nose bone.**
*Photo by Shawn Frederick*

# BMX

**BMX star Rick Thorne is airborne as he does the showy vertical tailwhip.**
*Photo by Shawn Frederick*

**Rick Thorne demonstrates his dexterity on the bike as he catches air during a wall ride X-Up.** *Photo by Shawn Frederick*

# IN-LINE SKATING

Brazilian aggro skating star Fabiola da Silva does a back side air. Because there are currently no aggro vert contests for women, da Silva is ready and willing to complete against men. *Photo by Jess Dyrenforth*

An unidentified streetstyle skater slides down a long handrail with amazing skill. *Photo by Jess Duyrenforth*

ridden. Though it sounds simple, streetstyle riders must have great balance and the skills to navigate almost anything.

- *Vert or vertical.* Vert skating usually refers to the half-pipe, and is an extremely popular form of the sport for riders and spectators. It is also a good way for professional riders to attain notoriety and make big money. Vert is one of the showcase events of the X-Games and a style of skating that allows riders to produce the biggest air and do the most spectacular tricks. Tony Hawk is probably the greatest star vert riding has ever produced and he still competes today.

- *Parks.* Skate parks offer something for both streetstyle and vert riders. The purpose of skate parks is the same today as when they first started: to give people a place to skate and hone their skills in both vert and streetstyle. Today's parks have a variety of special ramps where skaters can get big air and do tricks. There are also streetstyle sections containing real and constructed objects to jump, ride, or grind across, allowing skaters ample ways to practice. A good skate park will have a little something for everyone.

## Basic Riding Skills

Before a new rider picks a style, or even decides what kind of skateboarder he wants to be, he has to know something about the equipment he will be using. As with almost any sport—alternative or traditional—the same basic rule of thumb applies: Buy quality equipment that is durable and made for the kind of riding you plan to do. Boards endorsed by professional riders and made by first-rate companies will provide this kind of quality. If you go cheap, you'll get cheap, and cheap equipment often does not allow you to perform up to your capabilities. You should be able to obtain reliable advice at a good sporting goods store or on the Internet.

The board part of a skateboard is called the deck. There are two general lengths of board, the traditional, or street board, which is under 33 inches, and the longboard, which is over 35 inches. Traditional decks are the most common and most versatile, used for almost all styles of the sport. Longboards are generally used for cruising only and give the rider an almost "surfy"

**The legendary Tony Hawk performing the difficult 900-degree spin.**
Photo by Rob Gracie

feel. As a general rule, younger and smaller skaters should choose shorter boards because they will provide greater control.

Deciding upon the width of the board is again a personal choice the skater must make. Street decks range in width between 7.5 inches and 8.25, although both wider and narrower boards can be found. Most decks today have a raised front (the nose) and back (the tail), as well as raised sides. This is called the concave. The deeper the concave, the more aggressive a skater can be while doing tricks. However, newcomers to the sport will be better off starting on a board that has a shallower concave.

Most boards are made from wood, with Canadian maple the most common type used in construction. The board is put together in layers, or plys, to give it flexibility and durability. There are usually no fewer than five plys and no more than nine. These are the best quality boards you can buy. There are less expensive boards made from plastic, which can be very durable, but they are less responsive to the rider. Recent experiments with aluminum and fiberglass/carbon composites may be the future of skateboard construction. Manufacturers are trying to find a way to improve upon the durability of wood decks while maintaining the same pop and responsiveness. As the sport continues to grow, the technology will no doubt keep pace.

Good advice about the trucks is very important because trucks attach the wheels to the board and will determine the kind of ride you get. Size is determined by deck width. A slightly wider truck will offer a more stable landing platform and shorter turning radius. Manufacturers continue to look for ways to reduce the weight of trucks while retaining durability. Wheels, too, can be purchased separately, to be fit to a particular set of trucks and then the deck. Customarily, smaller wheels (52–60 mm) are used for streetstyle and the pipe, while larger wheels are used with the longboard. The urethane wheels have different degrees of hardness and thus have a hardness rating, as measured by a durometer. Any wheel with a reading above 90 on the durometer is considered hard. The harder the wheels, the more pop a skater can get, but the harder he will land.

## A Word About Safety

When a skateboarder flies out of the half-pipe and tries to do a spinning, tumbling trick in the air, there is always a chance he will be injured upon landing. When a street skater tries to slide down a handrail, he can lose his balance, fall, and be hurt. There's no way a skateboarder will stay injury-free all the time. The more tricks he tries to do or the faster he tries to go, the greater chance of an injury. There are a few pieces of safety equipment that can and should be worn always.

- *Helmets.* Helmets must be worn by all skaters at all times, regardless of their ability level. This is the best and only way to prevent head injuries. Helmets should always fit securely and be buckled or fastened. A rider should never buy a helmet that shifts on his head when his head moves. The front of the helmet should come down to a finger's width above the eyebrows. Bike-style helmets made from expanded polystyrene offer the most protection on impact. However, they must be replaced after every impact.
- *Knee pads.* Knee pads are important for all skaters, but especially for beginners. Make sure the pads fit correctly and are fastened securely around the leg. Pads usually come in three sizes—small, medium, and large, according to body size.
- *Elbow pads.* Elbow pads are always recommended for beginners, as well as for all aggressive skaters. As with knee pads, they come small, medium, and large.
- *Wrist guards* and *gloves.* Both beginning and advanced riders should wear some kind of hand protection while on their boards. Some wrist guards are made with a hard plastic splint, inserted to give the wrist added protection in case of a fall.

## Cruise Before You Fly

It isn't difficult to learn the basics of skateboarding. Once a rider is up on the board, he can learn some simple maneuvers quickly. How far he goes from there depends on the amount of time he practices and rides his board. For beginners, there is one very basic rule of thumb: Stay on the ground. Cruise before you fly. Don't try anything that will take you airborne until you are completely at ease and secure while riding and maneuvering the board on the ground.

A rider can propel himself as he would on an old-fashioned scooter. The front foot (whichever feels more comfortable, right or left) should be placed on the board over the front trucks and the back foot a bit over the tail. Then, lift the rear foot and push the ground. Once the board is moving, put the rear foot back on the board and feel balanced as you cruise in a straight direction, weight over the center of the board, knees bent, and hands low and extended out on each side. Once a rider is comfortable doing this, he can learn to steer the board.

Steering is done by leaning back and forth with the body and also by pivoting the feet with slight pressure toward the toes or heels. These are not overt movements and don't take great effort. Much depends on the rider's sense of balance and the tightness of the trucks. Beginning riders should make sure that the trucks are tight. It shouldn't take long for a rider to learn to steer his board by shifting his weight and leaning. He'll find that his control of the board increases rather quickly.

The following are a number of other maneuvers done on the ground which will enable the rider to have more control over the board and to prepare him for some basic tricks.

- *The kickturn.* The kickturn is a way to turn the board by lifting one set of wheels and pivoting over the other end's trucks. By lifting and pushing the end of the board around, a rider can make a turn of any angle. This may be done in either a frontside or backside direction. Step behind the trucks opposite the end of the board you want to lift; shift your weight to bring up the end. Then, using your hips, arms, and legs, swing the board in the direction you want it to go. It should pivot on the wheels that remain in contact with the ground. Once again, good balance is the key, but this maneuver usually comes easily to new riders.
- *The 180.* The 180 is an extended version of the kickturn in which the rider is ends up facing the opposite direction. The principle is the same.

The rider should get up on his rear wheels, then pivot the board by swiveling his hips and moving his arms in the direction he wants to pivot.

- *The 360.* This resembles the 180, except the rider does not stop half-way around. He will end up in the same position in which he began. Sometimes riders will stay balanced on the rear wheels and see how many 360s they can do without setting the board down. Before aerials began, successive 360s were always a challenge and showed how much control riders had over their boards.

- *GI Joe.* In this one, the rider stands with both feet perpendicular to the length of the board. He then moves each foot out to the end beyond the trucks. From there, the maneuver is done by raising one truck, then setting it down in front of where it had been, then repeating with the other. The rider should not take his foot off the board. By repeating the maneuver, he can walk the board in a forward direction.

- *Space walk.* In this maneuver the rider lifts the front trucks off the ground, then swings the nose from side to side without allowing it to touch the ground. It's almost like a dance, and the wider you can swing, the better it looks. Mastering this maneuver will make it easier for the new rider to start working on the manual.

- *The manual.* This is akin to riding a wheelie on a bicycle or motorcycle. The rider begins by skating in a forward direction, then lifting the front end of the board and rolling on the back wheels. It is performed through balance, by leaning back and lifting the front trucks. The balance a rider achieves by being able to manual for a distance will help when he moves on to other maneuvers. Riders should make sure, however, that they don't drag the tail of the board during the move because they can chip it up.

- *Acid drop.* This maneuver will prepare a rider for initial forays into the air. It is done merely by the rider standing still and holding the board in one hand. Then, he jumps high into the air, lifts his knees to his chest, and puts the board quickly under his feet—wheels down, of course. As he comes down, the rider should let go of the board, straighten his legs, and land squarely with his feet over the trucks. Knees should be bent upon impact for balance and to lessen the shock. This one may take practice, but it will help a rider get ready for the next level.

## Starting to Catch Air

There is a maneuver, considered simple and basic today, which changed the face of skateboarding because it allowed riders to get into the air without losing contact with the board. It is called the ollie and was invented by Alan Gelfand in 1978. Every serious rider has to know how to ollie and should practice it diligently. Once a rider has mastered the ollie and some other basic air tricks, he'll be better prepared to concentrate on the style of the sport he likes the best.

- *The ollie.* To set up the ollie, the rider places his back feet on the tail of the board and his front feet in the middle. To start the maneuver, he pops down with his back feet, so that the tail of the board hits the ground. Just as the tail hits the ground, he must slide his front feet up to the nose and jump. This will level the board and bring it off the ground. If you are jumping off something, try to land straight and with your feet over the trucks. The ollie takes practice. It is a snappy motion, but still a smooth one. It can be used to jump over objects and land the rider safely, something once thought nearly impossible on a skateboard since the feet are not attached. Sometimes the back foot will come off the board a bit as the rider goes into the air, but he or she should always land with both feet on the board and in the same position as when the maneuver began.
- *The nollie.* This is almost a reverse ollie. The front foot is moved to the nose of the board and the back foot is at the middle. This time, the rider pops the front foot down and slides the back foot to the tail of the board. If a rider brings his knees up as he makes the move, he will go even higher.
- *The kickflip.* This one at first sounds difficult, and requires some practice. The rider begins as if doing an ollie, except that the front heel is hanging off the board. Some riders prefer to place their foot at a 45-degree angle. Then they pop down on the back of the board and slide their front foot up, flipping the board with the side of their foot, just in front of the trunks. The riders go up in the air as the board flips over. If they stay above the board they should land back on it after it has flipped. Again, this takes timing and practice, and is one of those technical tricks where the rider doesn't move much.

**Skateboarder CaraBeth Burnside demonstrates one way of doing an ollie transfer.** Photo by Rob Gracie

- *Frontside 180/360.* This is another move that will get a rider in the air. It's not an easy trick to do on flat ground, so it's best to find a drop, even if it's just a high curb. Speed is required for the maneuver as the rider approaches the drop, then ollies and turns by putting weight on the back as he pops the board. For a 360, the rider should put the foot further back and turn even faster. Make sure you have your protective gear on. If you don't land straight, you may fall.

Once skaters do these basic maneuvers, they're ready for more advanced tricks. They can start to ollie up on objects like a bench, ledge, or rail, and then grind (slide) across them before jumping down. Or they can begin to ollie over obstacles. The stronger a skater becomes, the bigger and higher the objects can be. Before long, the rider has excellent control of the board for skating, turning, jumping, grinding, ollieing, and spinning, all the while remaining on the board.

Fun is the reason so many skaters prefer streetstyle. Because it can be done almost anywhere (that is, where skating isn't prohibited), riders can always find objects to jump over or slide across. There are even streetstyle competitions on courses set up to emulate obstacles found on the streets.

"The courses are often elaborate setups with speed and flow built in," Dave Duncan explained. "Competitors can do tricks on each obstacle. They are built for both the speed and style riders, as well as the technical riders. Some prefer to fly around fast, while others go more slowly and do more complex tricks. The technical skater will usually get more points, but only if he isn't too boring to watch.

"Courses have ramps, which offer speed and style, ledges and rails for the more technical maneuvers, and a mixture of radius ramps and flat banks. Everything is built to simulate things on the streets, such as rails, handrails, and benches. It is meant to be challenging, but not so difficult that riders can't do standard tricks. Competitors have two days to ride the course before they actually compete, so it has to be easy enough for them to adapt to it. Each course on the competition circuit has a different paint or look, and different designs. That's the nice thing about street obstacle courses. There are no rules for designing. You can do your own thing."

Duncan also observed that so-called "junk" courses are constructed where kids can skate just to have fun. "With junk courses they take old stuff like file cabinets, wood pallets, and plywood, and maybe lean the plywood against an old refrigerator. You can create a junk course for very little money but they are fun to ride. It's almost like a kid setting something up behind a shopping center. It has the urban street look to it. Add some construction-type signs and trash cans, old fire hydrants and road hazard signs, and you've really got something. You try to make it look junky, raw, and urban, and that way you keep the sport from being too clean and polished, and retain the old traditions."

Dave Duncan loves the idea that street courses and skate parks are springing up again. He enjoys designing them because they provide the opportunity to be different and creative. In his opinion, most parks can be set up on about an acre of land. A competition street course might be just 100 x 100 feet with some as large as 150 x 150 feet. Recreational courses, depending on budget, can be about 100 x 100 feet, often with separate areas for beginning, intermediate, and advanced skaters.

"Some of the parks have what we call snake runs," Duncan said. "It almost resembles a bobsled track, with big S-turns in it. Of course they are smaller and not as fast as a real bobsled run, but they often go right into a big bowl where the skater can carve around, do tricks, and have a lot of fun. They still put concrete pools in the skate parks, as well. Some are kidney shaped, others round. Many have a deep and a shallow end, just like a real swimming pool, with walls like vertical ramps. Everything is smooth and can be ridden."

In other words, there is something for everyone, fun for everyone, and the opportunity for riders to skate as if they were on the street and using natural terrain. The new skate parks manage to retain the flavor of the street and help the sport reflect its roots.

## Half-Pipes As Well

Because of their increasing popularity, half-pipes are now being constructed in recreational skateparks. "There are different sizes for varying degrees of skill," Dave Duncan explained. "The six-foot-high ramp is the mini-size, the eight-foot is considered a mid-ramp, while four feet or less is micro, for small children and beginners. Most skate parks should have these."

In some parks, rails, bars, and even picnic benches are located at the top of vertical ramps. That way, skaters can come out of the ramp and do additional tricks on the top. "A lot of the stuff done on the streets, with kids riding rails and ledges, is now being done with the vertical, as well," Dave Duncan said.

In the 1990s, Duncan explained, two skaters, Colin McKay and Danny Way, were most responsible for bringing streetstyle tricks to the vertical. "These guys began doing flip tricks and using obstacles on the top," Duncan said. "They both became world famous in their teens, but introduced these innovations when they were in their twenties. In a sense, they took up where Tony Hawk left off. Hawk has his signature moves, but McKay and Way, who still compete, have done things Tony never did, even though he has spanned all the generations. Rune Glifberg, who in 2001 was ranked the number-one vertical rider in the world, says he was heavily influenced by McKay and Way."

The parks normally do not have competition ramps since they might be dangerous for skaters without the skills. Today, competition ramps (the half-pipe) are usually between 40 and 64 feet wide. According to Dave Duncan, today's vertical ramps offer many options. Some may have a "roll-in," which is six feet higher than the normal deck. The starting point puts the skater up higher so he can roll down a steep bank and get up more speed. In this way, his first air can be 10 feet high and first few tricks can be done 8–10 feet in the air.

While streetstyle continues to dominate the sport, more riders are getting into the half-pipe and vertical riding. Much of that attraction is the result of television broadcasts, such as those of the X-Games, which have brought vert riding to the American public, and more sponsors (and more prize money) to skaters. Many young riders are in a hurry. They want to go for the prizes and glory of vert riding. But for every world-class vert rider, there are thousands of amateur skateboarders enjoying the sport, skating streetstyle and keeping the parks full.

Either way, today's riders are having a skateboarding blast as never before. You can watch the tricks and maneuvers, but if you look closely, you'll see the smiles of the riders, as well.

# 8

## Let's Talk Half-Pipe

Talk about the spectacular in skateboarding and you'll likely be talking about vert riding. Catching air, especially in the half-pipe, has become synonymous with notoriety, adoring fans, big prizes, and major endorsements. Young skaters, wanting to make a name for themselves, will invariably decide to ride the half-pipe.

As with the same venue in snowboarding, riders fly out of the pipe and do some amazing tricks in midair. In the minds of some, it's even more difficult on a skateboard because unlike snowboarding, the rider's feet are not attached to the board. Yet today's riders are doing more difficult variations of traditional tricks, flying higher and spinning more as they try to find their own special niche in the sport.

To get a better perspective on half-pipe competitions, let's take a look at two generations of riders, starting with the living legend, Tony Hawk.

### What's a Tony Hawk?

It may be the perfect name for a guy who loves to fly. Had Tony Hawk's name been "Benjamin Smith," he still would have been a champion and one of the giants of his sport. But . . . Tony Hawk! How better to conjure the image of flying through the air? Arguably, Tony Hawk is to skateboarding what Babe Ruth is to baseball, Joe Montana to football, or Michael Jordan to basketball. He is the man who set the standard for his sport, so much so that more kids today know his name than that of nearly any other professional athlete.

As a child, Tony Hawk was athletic and aggressive. Still, he couldn't seem to find the right sport. He played tennis and swam early, tried baseball and basketball, but like many athletes in alternative, individual sports, he couldn't get into the spirit of traditional team sports. Tony's older brother, Steve, was a skater, and when he went off to college, he gave his old, fiberglass skateboard to his younger brother.

Living in California, Tony went to the old Oasis Skatepark in Mission Valley. Thin and small at the time, he had to keep out of the way of older skaters, but before long he found something that would allow him to express himself as an athlete—doing it on his own and being as aggressive as he liked without worrying about alienating teammates. Hawk skated so hard that he became a regular at the local emergency room for treatment of assorted injuries.

Tony entered his first contest at the age of eleven, and by the time he was in high school he was practicing at the Del Mar skate park, had turned pro and already found sponsors, and was traveling with them to competitions in other states. At that time, however, skateboarding was still thought of as a nowhere sport, with few top riders.

"It was such a small scene then," Hawk said. "The events in which we competed had maybe 100 or 200 people watching. Turning pro back then wasn't exactly something grand."

Before he finished high school, however, skateboarding was entering one of its boom periods and Hawk was beginning to stand out. He grew tall and muscular. His style, at the time, was called circus skating because of his propensity for finesse and tricks as opposed to speed and power, which tended to dominate the sport. But soon styles began to change, with more riders using finesse to develop their tricks, and Tony Hawk became a star. At the end of 1983 he was declared the first National Skateboard Association champion. It wouldn't be the last time he was accorded that honor.

By the end of his high school days, Hawk was already earning in the neighborhood of $70,000 a year, owned a home, and had been in a national commercial for Mountain Dew. But, by the early 1990s, when skateboarding was in one of its temporary declines, Tony's wife Cindy was earning more money as a manicurist than he was as a world champion skateboarder. He recalled a demonstration in Japan during that period attended by fewer than thirty people. It was hard to believe then that within ten years, Tony Hawk would be one of the most famous athletes on the planet.

Things began to change with the 1995 X-Games, where Hawk was a standout. Over the next few years, his amazing skills and tricks in the half-pipe became legend. Yet, there was one trick that had eluded him: He wanted to be the first skater to successfully land the 900. To do that, the skater has to ride up the wall of the pipe, go high enough to make a pair of 360 rolls, then do a final 180 before landing. Hawk tried it first in France in 1986 and didn't make it. Another attempt in 1997 resulted in a cracked rib and another failure.

As great as Tony Hawk was, he admitted that trying the 900 had become somewhat frightening. "There's always an element of fear when you try something new," he said. "But you have to keep going at it with confidence."

However, whenever he practiced the 900 he wound up with more bumps and bruises than the last time. But he wouldn't quit. "About a year later," he said, "I began working on how to shift my weight while spinning to get my body in the right position to land." At last, he began to feel he was mastering the difficult maneuver. Then, at the 1999 X-Games in San Francisco, Tony Hawk would fly as never before. He waited until he was ready, launched himself off the ramp and went into his roll. Once, twice, then another 180! The crowd went wild.

Tony Hawk had become the first skater to land a 900!

Today, Hawk continues to be an icon of his sport and "Tony Hawk's Pro Skater" is one of the most popular video games ever made. At the age of 35, Hawk still competes occasionally and maintains an amazing command of his board. Most likely, he has earned more money than any other skateboarder, possibly more than many traditional athletes. Yet what pleases him most is that his sport has found universal acceptance.

"There's always been a negative stereotype with skating because people didn't really take the time to understand it," Hawk has said. "Now they realize that skateboarding can positively impact kids. It's athletic and artistic, and really is a positive outlet. The fact that events like the X-Games have been happening and growing bigger has helped that perception.

"It has been crazy," he continued. "I never dreamed it would be that successful. Suddenly we're not struggling to skate full time. We're not struggling to be accepted or recognized. Now you can go out and tell people you're a pro skater and they're interested, instead of saying, 'Is there such a thing?'"

## A Superstar for Today

No one would have predicted that Rune Glifberg, born in Copenhagen, Denmark, in 1974, would grow up to become a skating star in the United States. Among his many honors, however, is being ranked the number one vert rider in 2001, the year he was the World Cup winner in skateboarding. He also won the 2000 Vans Triple Crown final in the vertical as well as the overall Vans Triple Crown title in 2001, with the most points. How Rune got to that lofty position is a story in itself, one which mirrors that of many top riders.

As a youngster, Rune played some soccer, the number-one team sport in Denmark, but he didn't care for team sports. At that time, there wasn't much skateboarding activity in Europe. Around the age of eleven, a friend of Rune's took a trip to Texas and returned with a skateboard. Rune borrowed the board, liked riding it, and saved his money to get one of his own. Early on, he always bought used boards from his friends.

"I liked the individual sports because there wasn't someone always telling you what to do," he said. "I found skating exciting, probably because it was fast and dangerous, and it was fun. It also seemed as if a great deal of skill was needed to become really good at it."

Young Rune saw a Danish skater named Nicky Guerrero, who was a professional at the time, with a United States skateboard company as his sponsor, and, he says, "Once I saw him skate I was hooked. He did a half-pipe demonstration in Copenhagen and the stuff he did was amazing. He was doing inverts and handstands in the pipe, five-foot airs with a strong, graceful style of riding. He made it look so appealing.

"That's what made me get into vert riding instead of street," Rune admitted. "Vert was more exciting at the time. Soon I began practicing in the pipe, just working my way back and forth. At first I couldn't even get to the top of the ramp. But less than a year later, I was dropping in from the

**Champion skateboarder Rune Glifberg.** Photo by Shawn Frederick

top and slowly trying to learn all the tricks. It was a real slow process. It was still a new thing and riders didn't progress that quickly. I think we were somewhat intimidated by the new tricks that were being invented and done then."

Times have changed. According to Rune, learning to skate the half-pipe is no longer such a slow process. "Young athletes today will try anything and get into it real fast," he said. "They skate for a year or two and can become top-level amateurs. So much more is available and they find inspiration by watching established skaters."

One difference then was that tricks that are all well known today were only being invented when Rune was learning to skate. "When you saw a new trick it took you a few years to really get it and be able to do it," he explained. "I was just learning at 11, 12, and 13. I used to ride hills a lot, going down hills fast for a thrill and to get the adrenaline pumping. You always have some scary moments when you're not really sure what's going to hap-

**Rune Glifberg catching air to do a frontside indy nose bone.**
**Photo by Shawn Frederick**

pen at the bottom. You're exploring your limitations, learning the basics, like how to ollie.

"But I loved it from the beginning, was really hooked. In the summer of 1990 there was a big competition in Copenhagen and a group of pros came over from the States. I was approached by an English guy who had a company called Deathbox. He asked me to ride for him as an amateur. Deathbox turned into Flick Skateboards in 1995, the same year the X-Games began. I still ride for them."

Because skateboarding wasn't yet big in Europe, Rune's dream was to move to the United States and help establish Flick Skateboards there. When the company expanded to America, Rune was one of four pro riders who came along, the same time Tony Hawk's Birdhouse skateboard company became the distributor for Flick, as well.

Rune Glifberg finally made real inroads as a pro when he won the Slam City Jam in Vancouver in 1996. "It was my first-ever pro win and it came

**Rune Glifberg flies high again to do a super tweaked learn air.**
Photo by Shawn Frederick

against all United States riders," he recalls. "I really didn't go there to win—didn't expect to win—but when it happened, it opened my eyes. Suddenly, there was no one else to beat. For the first time in my life there was no next level. I was there, and it gave me the confidence to keep going, to push myself to be one of the top skaters on the circuit. I wanted to prove to myself that I could do it again and again and again."

Learning the pipe is one thing, but getting to the top and staying there is another. For Glifberg, that means constant practice, but with purpose and not with reckless abandon.

"I practice all the time, but I don't have a set routine," he explained. "My philosophy is to skate as much as possible, but at the same time to be careful not to push too hard. You've got to find a balance so you can go hard and not injure yourself, yet make sure you continue to improve. If you push too hard and always get injured, you'll go backwards. You must know your limits and can't try things you're not ready to do. Your skill level has to develop naturally and if you let that happen, you'll make progress.

"If you think you're one step ahead of yourself, you can be injured and go back three steps. Sometimes I'll try a new trick twenty or thirty times and I won't make it. That tells me I'm not ready, and I might leave it alone for six months to a year before trying it again. By then, I hope my skills will have developed to the point where I can make it. With skating in the half-pipe you have to learn to crawl before you walk."

Although Glifberg says that some young athletes learn rapidly and can do some amazing tricks very quickly, others have to work on the same thing for five or ten years. Many young skaters today, he predicts, can be fooled by what they see in magazines or on videos.

"Young skateboarders will see these tricks being done and want to go out and do them immediately," said Glifberg. "What they don't realize is that the guy doing the trick might have been skating for twelve or fifteen years, while they've been skating for only two. Newer skaters also see older guys making good money and they want to rush so that they can, too. A few have astonishing natural talent and can do a trick, but others don't quite have that talent yet are determined to try. They're the ones who get hurt. The drive for money or fame drives them to move faster than their capabilities."

Glifberg said that the most common injuries in skateboarding are knee problems, including such major ones as torn anterior cruciate ligaments

(ACLs). Many occur, he said, when skaters misjudge landings or the way they slide down on their knees when they don't make a trick. Although he has skated at a world-class level for years, he claims he's been lucky with injuries, having suffered no major knee problems. His most severe injury has been a broken ankle, which he received in Germany while practicing.

"It was at a new park and I was excited about skating there and didn't warm up properly," he recalls. "I tried a trick, didn't make it, and stepped off the board the wrong way, twisting my ankle and causing the break. Obviously, as a professional skater you want to stay healthy and not be out of action for long."

Riding in the half-pipe requires you to be creative with your tricks. "We try to make up our own by combining known tricks in ways they haven't been done before."

Glifberg has competed during a period in which the half-pipe itself has become larger. Ramps, he explains, used to be ten or eleven feet high. Today's standards are about thirteen feet, with eleven-foot transitions and a two-foot vert. "The old pipes had nine-and-a-half-foot transitions and a foot and a half vert," he said. "When I was younger we rode ramps that were fifteen feet wide. Today, we don't skate less than sixty feet wide."

Glifberg also says that styles in the pipe have changed somewhat over the years. "Street skaters, as a rule, don't use their hands," he explained. "But that's harder for vert skaters because they have been used to grabbing the board. Today, the skaters work to fine-tune their skills with their feet. A lot of the grabs are still around, grabs that were invented back in the 1980s. In vert, it is sometimes necessary to use the grab, but today most tricks work better if you don't grab. In essence, when you use your hand the purpose is to help out the trick, to make it easier. Some grabs, however, are necessary to pull you in a certain direction or to make your body twist, and the grab is the only way to keep you in contact with the board.

"When Tony Hawk invented all the 540 tricks, even the basic 540 spin, they were always done with a grab. When he finally did it without a grab it was considered one of the most amazing things in skateboarding ever. Even other riders couldn't believe it. Nowadays, a lot of the tricks done in the pipe and in vert skating look better if you can do them without your hands. Snowboarding is different. Riders are attached to their board, but still do the grabs. For the most part, the grab adds style in snowboarding and I think

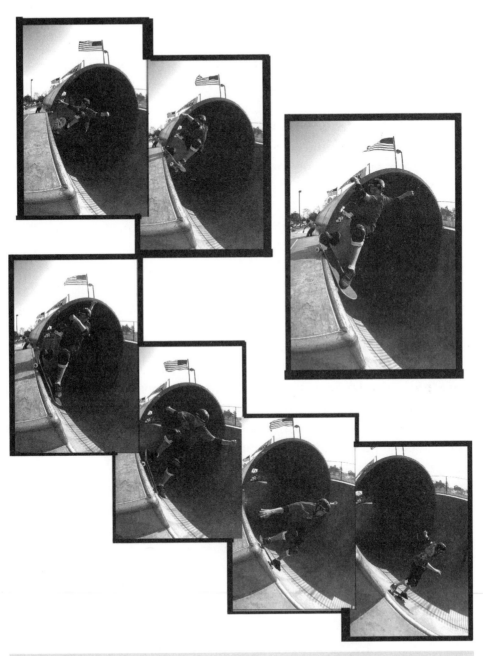

**Rune Glifberg shows the moves needed to do the smith grind.**
Photo by Shawn Frederick

some snowboarders feel that the trick is more difficult with the grab. In skateboarding, it's the other way around."

Glifberg himself does a very difficult trick without a grab, one that might be easier if he did grab the board at one point.

"It's called a kickflip to backside lip slide," he explained. "To do it, you have to come up the ramp forward and do a kickflip, turning the board below your feet as you come to the top of the ramp. After the board flips, it has to land on the top of the coping. You then have to come down on the board and do a 180-degree turn, slide along the top of the coping with the front wheels inside the ramp and the back wheels on the platform, then start down the ramp again. It's highly technical and it doesn't involve using your hands to grab the board."

The half-pipe events are surely the most spectacular in skateboarding. Specialty events, such as big airs and most-spectacular-trick, also rarely fail to impress. They are also the events that beg the most television coverage and involve accordingly the most prize money and sponsorships. Only the very best of the best vie for the championships, though a bevy of young skaters are hoping to make their marks in the upcoming years.

"Vert skating is definitely most popular among mainstream skaters and the media now," Rune Glifberg said. "It's easier to understand and looks more spectacular. Street skaters have a greater tendency to fall, but the core kids are definitely more into street skating than vert."

Dave Duncan, who includes ramps and half-pipes when he designs skate parks, builds pipes geared to the ability of the riders, with smaller ramps for beginners and intermediates. He, too, acknowledges just how spectacular the world's best riders have become.

"Competition ramps are for the best skaters in the world," Duncan said. "It takes big speed and big air to make these ramps come alive. They're too big for most younger skaters. But the pros fly higher and further. They really know how to harness the power."

# 9

## More and More Contests

Contests have become the measuring stick for skateboarders to test their skills against others. While the X-Games and Gravity Games continue to have the greatest marquee value among skateboarding contests, the sport has grown to the point where contests abound in various countries throughout the year. Dave Duncan, who serves as a judge at many major skateboarding contests, still competes as well, although he is approaching his forty-first birthday.

"Yes, I'm still competing," he said. "Recently I had hip surgery to restore my full range of motion and the doctors tell me I'll be able to do everything I used to do. It wasn't traditional hip replacement; they didn't take away much bone. The surgery was intended to make the joint more flexible so I'll be able to compete again. They have a master's division for those age thirty and up, and now a grand masters division for those thirty-seven and up. Tony Hawk is in his mid-thirties and still competing, in addition to doing many demonstrations.

"I still enjoy the ride. I do it for the young skaters who are coming up. I will sign autographs, and talk to youngsters about the sport. That's one of the ways I can give back and contribute to my sport."

Duncan estimates there are now more than 500 professional skateboarders throughout the world. Most open events will have about 100 pros competing, rarely higher than 120. Major venues such as the X-Games and Gravity

Games accept the top twenty riders in vert and top twenty in streetstyle, based on rankings drawn from how well the riders fared in other major contests. According to Duncan, up to 160 riders compete each July at the World Championships in Germany, representing more than forty countries. It is perhaps the longest running skateboarding event, having been held for more than twenty years. Another major event, the Vans Triple Crown championship, is held at several different sites in the United States, with riders coming from all over the world to compete.

"It's an honor to win any of them," Duncan said.

There are also events specifically for women. Ride Like a Girl is a Canadian contest which first took place in Toronto, Ontario, in August 2002, while the All Girl Skate Jam, originally an annual event, has evolved into an international tour with contests held in Newport, Rhode Island; San Sebastian, Spain; and San Diego, California; as well as in Australia, Brazil, and Hawaii.

World Cup skateboarding schedules events across Europe, the United States, Canada, and South America, from March through November, and the Grand Prix of Skateboarding takes place every other summer in Lausanne, Switzerland. In addition, amateur contests for skateboarders of all ages are sponsored throughout the world. As proof that skateboarding has truly become a major international sport, a perfect example would be the 2002 X-Games, where a pair of Brazilians, Rodil de Araujo, Jr., and Wagner Ramos, finished first and second in streetstyle competition, with Kyle Berard of Virginia Beach coming in third. In vert (the half-pipe), Canadian Pierre-Luc Gagnon was the winner, with Brazilian Bob Burnquist in second place and Dane Rune Glifberg third. In Street Best Trick competition, Araujo and Ramos were again in first and second places, with Dayne Brummet of San Diego third.

## About the Judging

Like other sports where the contestants' style, skill, and creativity each help determine the winner, judging can be subjective. It's not exactly equivalent to crossing the finish line first, or having the best time on the clock, or a team scoring the most runs or most points. It is imperative that judges in

**CaraBeth Burnside flies high while doing the air to fakie.** Photo by Rob Gracie

skateboarding know the sport well and have a complete understanding of the tricks so they know precisely what they are watching.

Dave Duncan began judging in the 1970s, when skateboarding was still in its infancy. Later, in 1987, during the summer after he turned pro, he suffered a broken ankle and was again in a situation to do some judging. As he grew older and began to build ramps and parks, he also began to announce and judge more competitions.

There are three main criteria for judging half-pipe competitions: consistency, flow, and difficulty of trick. Each judge may look for something slightly different, though they have to be pretty much on the same wavelength.

"Judges usually meet before a competition," Duncan said, "and the one thing you all agree you're looking for is the difficulty of the maneuvers. You

**Rune Glifberg again, in a sequence demonstrating the skills needed for the kick flip indy air.** Photo by Shawn Frederick

**Mike Frazier goes up the half-pipe to do the alley oop indy nose bone.**
Photo by Shawn Frederick

want to see creativity and innovation, the latest techniques, tricks, and combinations. Then you look for speed, style, and consistency. The rider has to stay on the board and combine a variety of the old and the new. It's an overall impression. Scoring is based on a total of points, 100 being perfect. If someone has a good run, the score is usually in the 80s. If it's a really good run the score is in the high 80s. If it's an amazingly great run, you could easily go up into the 90s, but you always leave room to go higher."

As a judge, Duncan knows he can't please everyone all the time. Because he knows all the riders personally, it sometimes can present a tricky balancing act.

"Riders can let their emotions get in the way," he admits. "They may feel they have done exactly the ride they wanted, but when you have to judge them against everyone else, they just might not have been the best. So there is always going to be some controversy over judging. Because we're trying to make it as fair as possible, we have engaged up to six judges and there has been talk about using seven in major events."

Duncan remembers an event back in the 1980s called the Vision Skate Escape, at which there were five judges. Two outstanding skaters were the clear favorites: Tony Hawk and Christian Hosoi. The ramp had what Duncan calls a mini-ramp spine connected to it so that riders had an additional means of getting in and picking up speed.

"As a judge," Duncan said, "I felt that Christian, with his speed and power and his lines, ruled that ramp. The two judges to my left had Tony winning and the two to my right had Christian winning. I was the guy whose vote decided who won. Christian was flying high so I don't think anyone had a problem with him as the winner."

That doesn't always make it easy. As in a boxing match, both competitors may believe they've won. A judge simply has to make his decision and stand by it. Requiring a thorough knowledge of the sport makes it imperative that judges also be skaters. Otherwise, they couldn't possibly have a feel for what it takes to do some of the more difficult maneuvers.

Duncan sees a difference in judging streetstyle as opposed to vert. "Street is getting so technical today, with the difficulty and combination of tricks being done. With vert, you know a rider is going to have four or five big tricks, and some filler, set-up-type tricks, but with street, these guys are just going from trick to trick. Also, falls don't count as much in streetstyle because the rider isn't losing valuable time as he would in a vert ramp. So street is a bit tougher to judge."

Contests are very important to both the riders and the sport. Without contests, it's unlikely there would be professional skaters. The establishment of a pro circuit and worldwide contests has spread the word about skateboarding and given young riders who want to compete a goal worth working toward. No matter what the sport, a competitor likes nothing more than to be called a champion.

# 10

## A Bright Future

If you are worried about the future of skateboarding, worry no more. It's probably safe to say that the days of wondering what will happen next are over. No more flow and ebb, no more sudden slowdowns where the industry almost dies, only to be revived and thrive again. Those early years of struggling for acceptance are over and done with. Sure, there will always be people who can't understand why kids are skating down streets or jumping over benches, who will continue to feel those riders shouldn't be there. But the venues for legitimate skating grow with each passing year.

Even in traditional sports, success didn't happen overnight. When the National Football League began in the 1920s, teams formed and folded just as quickly. Some franchises didn't even complete the season before disbanding, and some of the fields on which they played wouldn't be good enough for a Pop Warner game today. The National Basketball Association wasn't founded until 1946, although there had been professional players for nearly forty years. Leagues came and went, or played on weekends only, and players made virtually no money. Put in the context of these traditional team sports, skateboarding has come a long way in a relatively short amount of time.

That begs another question: What comes next? At age 28, Rune Glifberg feels that he is already part of the older generation of skateboarders, one that will make it easier for young skaters to follow and expand the boundaries of the sport.

"My daughter is a year and a half now," he said. "I'll be supportive of anything she wants to do. I see parents with kids from five to ten years old, bringing them to skate parks, giving them boards and all the equipment they need to get started—coaching them, too, which makes learning even easier. All this tells me that skateboarding is a real sport now."

Dave Duncan also sees the sport opening up for more and more skaters. "More girls are skateboarding now," he says, "and more people riding longboards. The longboards, which measure thirty-six inches and more, allow older people to go out and cruise. A bigger variety of boards is available and I think you're going to see more parks built and more girls entering competitions. More competitions will spring up, prize money will grow, ramps will be bigger and street courses better. All this will lead to more TV exposure and more sponsors. For a long time it was only ESPN, but now NBC and Fox are beginning to cover events."

Duncan agrees with Rune Glifberg that the sport has now bridged the generation gap. "Parents are encouraging their children to ride, as long as they put on their safety gear," he said. "There are people on city councils whose kids ride skateboards, and they know they need parks for them."

As for the pros, Duncan observes them bringing the sport to new levels. "I thought I had seen everything in tricks ten years ago," he said, "but now there's a whole bunch of new varieties. Video games like "Tony Hawk's Pro Skater" game have helped—you can see a kickflip into a crooked grind and then you shove it out. Now riders themselves are doing that. The pros are becoming so consistent with their tricks that you are seeing all kinds of new things. The degree of difficulty of the tricks is amazing."

This veteran of the skateboarding wars also envisions the venues improving. "We can always build better street courses," he said, "and do more to the vert ramps, adding hips and bowls. I see us adding obstacles, for example, on the vert ramp like ledges and rails that will help bring that street technology up to the vert. The same goes for street, trying to simulate more of the real street with rails and ledges to produce a presentation of skating true to the sport. One of these days we'll get it just as we like it and the way it ought to be."

**Mike Frazier again, doing a body varial.** Photo by Shawn Frederick

That comes from someone who has always been true to his sport. Dave Duncan doesn't want skateboarding ever to lose its roots or its history. It was a street sport from the start and a street sport when it was barely tolerated in most places. Despite difficult times, no one could completely stamp out the core riders, the young skaters who took to the streets and wouldn't be denied. You don't forget about the rough times just because there are good times today.

"It's really so big now that nothing can stop it," Duncan concluded. "I don't think you'll again see the highs and lows we had to live through. Those days are gone. Now, skateboarding is a multibillion-dollar industry, complete with boards, shoes, publications, contents, even the fashion. There are many jobs available within the industry for those who can't be champion skaters—team managers, designers, and advertisers, all things that didn't exist when I was young."

Then Dave Duncan made a very simple statement, one which may sum up a fundamental reason why skateboarding is here to stay:

"More kids in America ride skateboards than play baseball. Skateboarding can be done anywhere, and it's a sport that builds confidence and character."

You can't put it any better than that.

# PART THREE

# BMX BIKING

# 11

# A Brief History

Today's world of BMX biking is wild and alive, bigger and faster than ever, and still growing. Riders are flying out of the half-pipe and off dirt ramps with increasing frequency, doing no-handed 540s, tailwhips, and no-footed can-cans—amazing, acrobatic tricks in the air which are the equal of those in snowboarding, skateboarding, or in-line skating.

Superstar riders, such as Dave Mirra, Rick Thorne, Cory Nastazio, and T. J. Lavin, have become heroes in the alternative sports world, professional riders who have mastered a difficult and demanding sport, one very exciting to watch. Years ago, no one could have envisioned bicycle riding being anything like this!

There was a time when bicycles were used mainly for transportation. Adults rode for exercise while kids rode back and forth to school, or might pedal to a friend's house or the local park looking to play another sport, such as baseball. Once in a while, two riders would take a dare and race each other. The older the rider, the bigger his bike, progressing from a starter bike, to 20 inches, to 24, and finally to 26- or 27-inch bikes.

There was a time when all bicycles were pretty much the same—big tires, foot brakes, and a single gear for riding. The development in the 1960s of a thin-wheeled "English" bike, one that had three gears, began to change the experience of riding. Lighter in weight and easier to ride, the gear shift made it less stressful to ride up hills. A ten-speed version appeared in the 1970s, and today's bikes may be fitted with eighteen gears or more. And, like automobiles, there are models and styles—from thin-wheeled touring bikes, to rugged, heavier-wheeled (and highly popular) mountain bikes, to bicycles built for two. Logic would dictate that the bigger the rider, the bigger the bike, until the biker is able to manage a full-sized touring or mountain bike.

However, people of all ages continue to ride a smaller bike, a durable 20-incher that can take a real pounding. In the 1960s, these 20-inch bikes (with 20-inch tires) became known as BMX bicycles. The reason was simple. Young athletes riding those bikes were beginning to emulate the motocross races—motorcycle races over a rough dirt course with hills and jumps. Thus, BMX stood for Bicycle Motocross. The X stands for the word "cross."

The sport, which originated in California during the mid-1960s, inspired young riders to race their bikes the way adults raced motorcycles. At first, most young riders were biding their time until they could graduate to motorcycles. Many parents, however, felt motorcycles were not only too dangerous, but too expensive. In the meantime, these kids spent so much time on their bikes that they began picking up new skills, making hills to jump and ride over, and showing amazing control of their riding. Soon, they were developing race courses with many other obstacles to enable them to race for fun.

One of the first organized races was held on July 10, 1969, at Palms Park in Santa Monica, California, which park attendant Ron Mackler helped set up. (Initially, the participants named the sport "Pedal Cross.") A year later, riders in Long Beach, California, also began to race, again copying the style of motocross. It was a clever thirteen-year-old named Scott Breithaupt who set up a dirt track on a lot and charged twenty-five cents admission. There were thirty entries in the first race, and once word got out the young riders flocked there. The second event had 150 entries. Breithaupt quickly saw the potential in this new sport and formed an organization called the Bicycle United Motocross Society (BUMS).

In 1971, more interest was kindled by the documentary movie *On Any Sunday*, which featured superstar Steve McQueen and focused on the world of motocross racing. Two years later, the National Bicycle Association (NBA) was founded by Ernie Alexander to organize and sanction these bike races. By that time, the sport had come to be known as bicycle motocross, or BMX, and more young riders became involved, following the urge to ride the track faster and better than those they were competing against. As with the other alternative sports, most of the first, radical riders were from California.

By 1974, it appeared that BMX was becoming firmly established, when *Bicycle Motocross News*, the first BMX magazine, was published in Orange, California, and the NBA held its first national competition at the Los Angeles Coliseum. There, Yamaha introduced the first BMX bicycle made for racing purposes, calling it the "moto bike," and offered $100,000 in prizes and promotion. *Sports Illustrated* covered the competition, giving it even more legitimacy.

This was all that was needed for the sport to migrate out of California. The National Bicycle League (NBL) was formed later in 1974 by George Esser of Pompano Beach, Florida. Also a sanctioning organization, the NBL was created in response to the feeling that the NBA focused only on California racing. The NBL soon began setting up dozens of tracks throughout the eastern part of the country. At the same time, European motocross riders visiting the United States brought the sport back to their home countries.

In 1977, a third sanctioning body was formed, the American Bicycle Association. That same year, BMX racing caught on in Australia, and three years later that country held its first national championships. In 1981, George Esser of the NBL met with interested parties from Canada, Columbia, Holland, Japan, Panama, and Venezuela to found the International BMX Federation (IBMXF), which sanctions international races, and established a world BMX championship.

It was during this time that BMX took a radical turn. Racing was still the main discipline practiced by BMX riders, but some free-thinking riders began doing new things on their own. Primarily racers, they started performing stunts on their bikes, tricks executed on flat land as well as catching air off jumps. Some riders, looking to sharpen their riding and stunt skills in other ways, sneaked into abandoned skateboard parks to ride the ramps and do street stunts not unlike those performed by skateboarders. Not surprisingly, one alternative sport once again influenced another.

Although many BMX racers looked down upon the stunt riding, freestyle

BMX wasn't about to die. In 1983, the manufacturer, Mongoose, began producing more rugged freestyle frames and a year later the first freestyle competitions were held, mostly in California skate parks. It was around this time that Rick Thorne found his way onto a BMX bicycle.

Born in Kansas City, Missouri, in 1969, Thorne began to ride in 1982. The sport had already spread to the Midwest, and Rick Thorne wasn't alone.

"We were a group of guys who rode," he said. "We called ourselves the BMX Brigade. There were maybe thirty of us and we would build ramps and tunnels, even try some quarter-pipe riding. The funny part was that everybody at school hated us."

As with skateboarders back then, kids who followed so-called alternative sports found themselves often isolated from the mainstream. As with many others, Rick Thorne couldn't take to traditional team sports.

"I just wasn't good at other sports," he recalls. "Riding gave me something that was mine, something that was personal. I think a lot of kids today feel what I felt twenty-two years ago in team sports. Back then, however, you played team sports or you played nothing. I had a bike at age twelve and soon I decided to jump and do tricks. We were always jumping curbs and doing wheelies, and people looked as us like we were a pain in the ass.

"Another part of it was that I didn't get along with many people growing up. I had some problems at home and got into riding because I needed an outlet for my anger. I felt free when I was on my bike. By the time I was thirteen I was already taking riding very seriously, and at fifteen I was touring and competing."

Not unlike many of these athletes, Rick needed something to call his own. Riding filled that need—one reason he continued to ride as he became older, when others his age were getting off their bikes and driving cars. "There were a number of reasons I continued," he said. "I enjoyed riding. I kept on setting new goals and I didn't limit myself to one style of riding. I also enjoyed going on the road and doing shows, and being around friends who liked the same thing."

In a sense, Rick Thorne was one of a group of youngsters who persevered at creating a new sport. He would later compete in vert events in the X-Games, Gravity Games, CFB Series, Vans Triple Crown of BMX, and the Soul Bowl—often placing in the top ten, which made him one of the best rid-

**BMX rider Rick Thorne.** Photo by Shawn Frederick

ers in the country—but back when he began, he and his friends were out there only to have fun.

"We would be out on the streets, getting in chases, jumping up stairs," Thorne said. "In the early 1980s there was no structure. No one knew what we were doing back then, and we were called outcasts and freaks because we didn't play team sports. At that time, there was nothing to strive for, no X-Games. We were on our own."

T. J. Lavin, born in Las Vegas, Nevada, in 1976, is a two-time X-Games gold medalist in dirt jumping. He has also won that event at the Gravity Games, and on two occasions has finished first at the King of Dirt competitions. At the beginning, he shared some of the same feelings as Thorne.

"I tried playing baseball and was the worst player on the team," Lavin said. "I also wrestled in high school, but wasn't great at that. Yet when I started riding a bike I had already taken off my training wheels by the time I was two years old. To be honest, I found baseball pretty boring. Standing in the outfield and waiting for the ball to come your way, you might as well be watching the grass grow. I never had that feeling on my bike. When I was riding, there was always constant action and we had a great time."

When T. J. Lavin was fourteen he and his friends began jumping and having neighborhood races on their bikes every weekend. A year later, he began going to a local track. "That's when I found out I was pretty good," he said. "I could go over jumps that others wouldn't take, but there was no dirt jumping back then, no way to enter a contest."

When he was sixteen, T. J. became friends with Nick Herda, who owned an appliance store in Las Vegas. He met Herda when he and his friends began riding on a track for four-wheel all-terrain vehicles (ATVs) located behind the appliance store. Herda caught them, but instead of being angry, he saw how passionate the kids were about riding. He decided to start a team called Herda's Hotshots, allowing them to race and practice in his backyard track every day. It kept them riding.

Like so many bike riders and skateboarders back then, T. J. Lavin was pressured by his family to get off his bike and strive for something else.

"My dad wanted me to go to college," Lavin said. "My mom said I had to start thinking about what I wanted to do in the real world. There was no money in BMX riding back then. Yet I would do anything it took to spend only a minute on my bike. I think if a person hasn't had that feeling, he might not understand what I mean. I loved being on the bike. It was almost crazy."

With riders like Rick Thorne and T. J. Lavin refusing to call it quits, the sport continued to grow. By 1985, sponsors were raising money for prizes and competitions expanded throughout the country. BMX boomed for about three years, but then the sport slowed down until the X-Games began in 1995. Stunt riding picked up again, with more riders taking to the disciplines. While BMX racing continued to grow during this period, it is estimated that only about 5 percent of BMX racers in the United States also do stunt riding.

Perhaps T. J. Lavin said it best when describing the growth of BMX riding. "It was a gift from God that they started the X-Games. The Games led directly to corporate sponsorships, rather than local sponsorships. And television coverage has helped immensely."

As with the other alternative sports, BMXing needed the X-Games and the broadcast coverage it provided. With that kind of stage on which to perform, other major venues and sponsors began to come the riders' way.

# 12

## The Freestyle Side of BMX

Getting on the bike and expressing their creativity—that was the joy of many young riders during the early days of BMX and the reason the freestyle forms of the sport evolved. Although the majority of BMX riders still prefer to race around tracks that mimic motocross tracks, stunt riding has grown tremendously since the first X-Games in 1995. The sport may not attract as many participants as, say, skateboarding, but hardcore riders such as Rick Thorne and T. J. Lavin have a love and loyalty for their sport which rivals any other. Stunt riding, or freestyle BMX, has evolved into four disciplines: dirt jumping, flatland, street, and vert.

1. *Dirt jumping.* Riders perform airborne tricks after taking off from a dirt ramp. There is no single size or shaped ramp. Some are larger than others, some more sloped. Contests are held on a "pack" of ramps, which is a series of various-sized ramps positioned so that the rider can establish a good rhythm as he goes off each one. During a contest, there are usually anywhere from three to twelve jumps in a pack.
2. *Flatland.* This is exactly the way it sounds. Riders perform acrobatics, using the bike as a kind of jungle gym, while slowly rolling over a flat surface or flat platform.
3. *Street.* This style is similar to the streetstyles of other sports. Riders perform stunts while jumping over boxes, rails, and pipes on a layout

**Dirt jumper T. J. Lavin goes inverted for this trick.** Photo by Shawn Frederick

not unlike one used for skateboarding. The course is set up to simulate riding around a town or city, doing tricks over any obstacles which might be in the way.

4. *Vert.* Another spectacular form of riding, vert stunts are performed within a half-pipe similar in shape and size to those used in skateboarding and snowboarding. Riders strive for big air and do some incredibly complex and often dangerous tricks. Interestingly, while BMX racing allows young riders to copy a similar form of motocross, the current sport of freestyle motocross (on motorcycles) evolved directly from the tricks done by vert riders on BMX.

## Getting Started

Though the disciplines of freestyle BMX generate the most excitement, there are some things all beginners must know to stay safe. After all, no one gets on a bike and immediately does big tricks. You have to ride before you jump. While most BMXers ride what is known as a 20-inch bike with 20-inch tires, the frames of these bikes can vary. There are mini, junior, pro, XL, and XXL frames, each tailored to the size of the rider. As a general rule of thumb, the size limits for the proper frame are as follows.

Young riders under 4 feet should ride a mini frame, those between 4' and 4'10" require a junior frame, and those who stand between 4'10" and 5'8" should ride a pro frame. Those between 5'8" and 6'4" need the extra large, or XL, frame, and any rider taller than 6'4" should get the largest, the XXL frame. Starter bikes can cost $85 and up. The better and harder a youngster rides, the better-quality bike he will need. The bikes have a single gear and should have hand brakes, not foot brakes.

Like many riders, Rick Thorne has his own signature line of bikes, so that young riders can identify with one of the stars of the sport. "Buy a lower-end bike at first to make sure you want to continue riding," he says. "Later, you can get a good bike for $250, which looks sharp and can be used for some rugged jumping. A top-of-the-line BMX bike can cost in the neighborhood of $1,000."

Some additional equipment is needed to ride safely. Beginners who have a tendency to try small jumps and new things should be sure to always wear

**BMXer Allen Cooke catches his share of the air while doing a no-hander-no-footer.** Photo by Shawn Frederick

their safety gear. Rule number one: Start with a high-quality helmet. This bears repeating: *Always wear a helmet!* If you feel your helmet has been damaged in a crash, don't take a chance. Get another one. Following is a list of the rest of the gear you will need and the reasons why.

- *Knee pads.* These are very important to protect the knees from conventional falls and bailouts when the bike is in the air.
- *Elbow pads.* Elbow pads help protect a rider when he doesn't clear a jump and goes down.
- *Shin guards.* This is an important piece of safety gear for riders who are catching air and starting to do no-footed tricks. They will prevent the pedals from floating back and cracking the rider's shin as he tries to get back on them.
- *Chest protector.* This may be something a rider associates with a catcher in baseball, but it has its place in BMX. Often used by the best riders doing the big air tricks out of the half-pipe or off a ramp, it protects them from the handlebars suddenly turning sideways and cracking them in the ribs.
- *Gloves.* Some look at gloves as optional, depending on the riding. They will keep a rider from developing blisters if the grips on the bike are worn. In addition, they will keep a falling rider from getting cuts and scrapes on his hands.

Obtain all these pieces of protective equipment before starting to ride. Clothing can be loose and comfortable. Riders should always wear long-sleeved shirts and long pants, so that minimal skin area is exposed in the event of a wipeout.

If you want to become a good freestyle rider, you have to stay on the bike, just as the pros do.

"The most fun I have is when I just ride," T. J. Lavin said. "Not competing in contests. Riding and doing anything I want. The real fun is inventing things, making your own series of jumps, building whatever you want and riding your own course. The more you ride and practice, the better you'll get."

Lavin confirms that young riders should always wear their safety equipment because injuries are going to be part of the game. "I always wear knee pads and, of course, a helmet," he said. "Probably the most common injuries in BMXing are wrist and ankle breaks on landings. All riders know they are going to be injured, but most have good hand-eye coordination and are able to avoid many crashes and injuries. It also helps if a rider does some trampoline work or takes some gymnastics lessons. Any kind of air awareness will help you as a rider, especially if you're going to be jumping."

Rick Thorne agrees with Lavin about injuries. He points out the vulnerability of knees and ankles in vert riding, and has himself undergone surgery on his knee and shoulder. "Most injuries stem from falls and impacts," he said. "Another not uncommon injury is concussion, getting knocked out. That's why a good helmet is so very important. I think we often look a lot more gnarly and aggressive than we actually are. Some people still feel that we are guys who don't care whether we get hurt. We still have the bad-boy rep and it just isn't true. My goal has always been to help people do something positive with their lives. I work just as hard as if I were a baseball or football player, so I feel good about myself, as most riders do. There is so much that is good in these sports. There is money to be made, but my heart is in the sport, not the dollar."

Though Thorne, like T. J. Lavin and others, likes nothing better than to be on his bike, he hates to use the word *practice*, though he knows that young riders must do a lot of it. He prefers to minimize the pressure and make practice informal. Many of the same things can be accomplished just by riding for fun.

"I ride different things at different times," he explained. "Practice for me is simply going out with my friends without any pressure and trying things. If you pressure yourself to improve or to conquer a particular discipline, you won't have fun. But if you are going to compete, you must have your tricks down pat before the season. On many occasions I learned things by riding with my friends, a kind of you-try-it and I'll-try-it thing. Every rider is different. I like to write my tricks down and then think about them."

T. J. Lavin has always specialized in dirt jumping and has become one of the best in the world. "You hit a series of jumps made of dirt and perform different stunts from jump to jump," he explained. "The contests are judged for height, style, and the difficulty of the tricks. Sometimes you don't even have a set routine—you make it up as you go along. If you catch a great backside on one jump (landing perfectly from the previous jump) it can give you maximum speed and height on the next, so you might do a trick requiring that kind of speed and height. If your landing is less than perfect and you can't get the speed up, you'll do a different trick."

Lavin began dirt jumping because the cost of practicing was minimal. He and his friends could build their own dirt ramps. He says he can ride the conventional ramps, but prefers dirt. Though he was largely self-taught, he feels young riders should seek help from someone who can advise and coach them. He'll often coach younger kids in his neighborhood who want to learn some basic tricks.

"I still ride a Schwinn, one of the oldest bikes in the country," he said. "You have to be sure your bike has the proper metals and welds. Sometimes it's trial and error to see what you prefer. Bikes evolve all the time, so a serious rider should choose the best bike he can afford and do it right the first time."

According to Lavin, dirt jumpers will sail about twenty feet in the air, with jumps ranging in length from fifteen to thirty-five feet. As with other sports, riders are developing more elaborate and difficult maneuvers on their bikes.

"When I look at my tapes from 1995 and 1996, I can't believe how the tricks have evolved," he said. "Last year's main-event tricks will barely get a rider into the finals of a major contest the following year."

Dirt jumping has never attracted huge numbers of participants. Lavin says there are only about fifty top dirt riders in the world, though many younger riders are drawn to the discipline with an eye toward competing. Lavin belongs to the first generation of dirt riders, since the discipline didn't come of age until the mid-1990s. According to him, there was a little bit of dirt jumping in the early 1980s, but racing and other freestyle forms were then much more popular.

"A guy named Tracer Finn was one of the original dirt jumpers," Lavin said. "He used to give demonstrations in the early eighties, and he was a wild guy. He would go off a jump and do a 360 in the air while pointing at the crowd. The problem was that he never really made a solid landing, he just went for the trick and crashed. He put his body on the line for the pleasure of the crowd. That was the mentality back then, and it still is, to some extent, except today's riders prefer to land correctly. I don't think anyone else ever did it quite like Tracer."

**T. J. Lavin goes airborne to do the difficult backflip off a dirt ramp.**
Photo by Shawn Frederick

Rick Thorne, whose background is similar to Lavin's, wound up gravitating to vert riding. It didn't happen overnight. Riding was the important thing at first. When he began touring at age fifteen, he would travel to state fairs, boat shows, and automobile rallies in order to do demonstrations.

"Flatland riding was more popular than ramp riding then," he says, "and street wasn't around yet. We would do flatland tricks and also ride in a quarterpipe, which was as it sounds, half the shape of a half-pipe. That was our ramp part, but flatland was looked upon as cool. In the early nineties, street and ramp became more popular and flatland faded into the background. I rode for fourteen years before I made a salary from it. I was a busboy at restaurants, paid for my own surgeries, and went to contests. Finally, in 1993, I quit my job when I was making enough at shows to pay my bills."

Doing tricks on the quarter-pipe led Thorne to compete in vert. "The half-pipe is more fluid and you can do a whole run, pumping one wall, then the other. Because the quarter is smaller, we did the tricks on one wall. We would do a trick, come back, get some speed and do another on the side wall, or same side of the pipe. You can do more on the half because you can build up speed. On the quarter, you can't go very high, so you are restricted, to some degree."

Thorne has noted that there is a sort of division among BMX riders that might exist in quite the same way in other alternative sports. There are two groups, which he calls the hardcore and the mainstream. Mainstream riders are those with big corporate sponsors, who compete regularly and always in major contests such as the X-Games. On the other hand, according to Thorne, hardcore riders have sponsors, make videos, and appear in the magazines that drive the industry.

"The hardcore kid doesn't want to go to the X-Games," Thorne explained. "They are riding just as hard as the mainstream guys, but in a different fashion. When they ride for the magazines, for instance, photographers want to see them doing new and technical tricks. They ride and get hurt as much as guys in the X-Games.

"Hardcore riders do flatland tricks and a lot of natural, downtown street riding. They do handrails, wall rides, curbs and ledges. And they ride in the skate parks. Actually, skateboarding and BMX are very close. They use the same terrain and the riders are like brothers. Many of the hardcores are great riders who deserve sponsors. I try to be a part of both worlds. I compete in vert and I'm seen on TV. But I love riding, and just because I'm on TV doesn't mean I can't ride and hang with the hardcores, as well.

"The hardcore kids are actually more involved in what's going on within the industry. They're more in tune with new products and fashion, they make videos, and they put time and effort into the presentation of BMX. In effect, the hardcore kids and the companies keep the sport grounded. If television were to disappear, everyone would be back to the magazines. The way I look at it, we should all help each other. I feel I'm on both sides of the fence, part of the mainstream and still one of the hardcore kids."

Thorne paints a picture of an entire BMX culture, a unified attempt to build a sport. BMX is not nearly as popular as snowboarding, skateboarding, or in-line skating, both in terms of total participants and big-time pro riders. Although most young people ride bikes, not that many have stayed with it long enough to develop the talent that leads to aggressive freestyle riding. But the numbers are increasing.

## Dave Mirra, Superstar

Dave Mirra is to BMX riding what Tony Hawk is to skateboarding: the most recognizable name in the sport. He started riding at the age of four, was jumping curbs and going off ramps a year later, and entered his first BMX freestyle contest at age ten. Today, Mirra has won nine gold medals, more than any other X-Games athlete. He competes regularly in street, vert, and vert doubles events. Like other top BMXers, Mirra got on a bike at an early age and never got off. By the time he graduated high school, he was a professional—one of the top ramp riders in the world, and named Freestyler of the Year in 1999 by *BMX Magazine*.

By virtue of his media exposure alone, Mirra was one of two alternative sports athletes to be recognized in 2000 as a "notable sports icon in all of mainstream sports." It was estimated that his media exposure had a value of approximately $2.5 million. In 2001, Mirra was voted BMX Rider of the Year at the first-ever ESPN Action Sports and Music Awards.

Mirra has a line of action figures created in his image, he appears on trading cards, has done TV commercials, and has a signature line of bikes and shoes. He has appeared on the cover of *Sports Illustrated for Kids,* and has

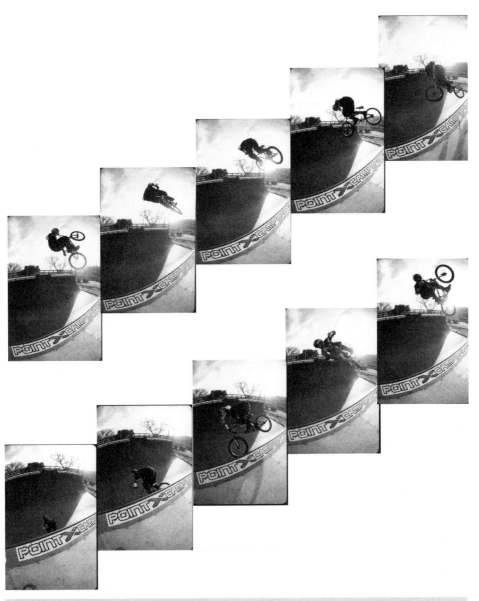

**In an exciting sequence, Rick Thorne demonstrates the vert ramp 540 spin.** Photo by Shawn Frederick

been featured in *Rolling Stone* and *ESPN the Magazine*. He has been a guest on *Good Morning America*, Disney's *The Jersey Show,* and *The Late Show with David Letterman*. According to Rick Thorne, this is exactly the way mainstream guys can pave the way for hardcore riders.

Another gauge of Dave Mirra's popularity is his ability to give back to BMXers in ways similar to contributions from stars of traditional team sports. He has started a Woodward Scholarship, which enables six young riders to spend a week at a BMX training facility camp in Pennsylvania, and he has been involved with the Make-a-Wish Foundation. Like so many other alternative sports athletes, Mirra credits the X-Games as the most important venue to have promoted the growth and proliferation of the sport.

"Television," Mirra asserts, "has allowed us to be seen as role models and is really the reason for success for any sport. I think it's awesome that ESPN went out and did something no one thought would be successful, and made it successful. It created a platform for us to show what we were all about, and it deserves thanks for bringing BMX to the mainstream.

In addition to his riding success, Mirra's high-profile image has been further enhanced by his video game, "Dave Mirra's Freestyle BMX," which is achieving the same kind of popularity as "Tony Hawk's Pro Skater" game. Mirra and young star Ryan Nyquist are the stars of the game, which focuses on tricks, stunts, and X-Games-style entertainment.

To make the game as realistic as possible, Mirra and Nyquist worked as consultants to provide accuracy and insight into court design and bike physics. The game features outstanding graphics and very intense trick details. It provides three courses users can challenge; street levels with ramps, stairs, and rails; dirt tracks, with bumps and jumps; and a big vert section. Like other realistic video games, this one can help show young riders how to do tricks and inspire them to continue their freestyle riding.

Dave Mirra has followed his own road to success, but like other BMX stars, it all began when he first got on a bike. His advice to young riders is to enjoy what they are doing and let the chips fall where they may.

"I have been riding my bike my whole life," Mirra said. "My heart was in it from day one. I didn't spend a lot of time thinking about turning pro. I just spent my time being the best bike rider that I could and stuck with it. Kids need to remember to start slow, have fun, and don't do anything that they are not capable of. That's the best way to stay healthy—stick to what you know you can do. Take your time and it will all happen."

## Riding Continues to Grow

From all indications, BMX freestyle riding is attracting more riders in the United States each year, and the sport seems to be taking off in England, where skateparks are springing up throughout the country for both skateboarders and BMX riders. British television has also served as a catalyst, as major events from the U.S. are shown in increasing numbers, as well as England's biggest contest, the Brickyard Jams.

English rider Jamie Bestwick has been making a major mark on the U.S. circuit, having won gold at the Gravity Games in 1999 and 2001, as well as an X-Games gold medal in 2000. Simon Tabron has also won at the Gravity Games and World Championships in 2002, and earned several medals from the X-Games. Alistair Whitton is another British rider whose star is on the rise. It is expected that more major events will be taking place in Britain in the next few years.

Freestyle BMX is fun, challenging, and exciting. It provides the rider with a healthful outlet and certainly gets him in good physical condition. As a sport, however, freestyle BMX riding is something that cannot be approached half-heartedly.

"I love to compete and train," Rick Thorne said. "I do the things any professional athlete does, train hard and eat right, stretch all the time, and take vitamins. I'm thirty-three now, and I feel I am riding the best I ever have. But it's still hard work."

Listening to riders like Thorne, Lavin, and Mirra, it becomes apparent that their kind of BMXing is a complete sport, requiring hard and careful training and preparation, and a willingness to sacrifice in order to excel. It can still be fun for recreational riders who don't want to go the extra mile, but the pros have shown that a relatively small, 20-inch bike, can be a vehicle for some of the biggest tricks in the sporting world.

# 13

## A Bevy of BMX Tricks

As is the case with the other individual sports, the incredible high-flying tricks done out of the half-pipe and off dirt ramps are the most exciting, eye-catching discipline in BMX. These tricks, of course, aren't for everyone, especially the difficult ones, but serious riders can learn a good many of them. Even those who bike for fun may challenge each other, make jumps and ramps, and see who can do the most. Magazines and videos introduce young riders to maneuvers they themselves can try. That's why safety gear is of the utmost importance, no matter how skilled you are.

Riders should also refrain from anything beyond the extent of their skill. That's the easiest way to get hurt. They should progress naturally, going from one maneuver to another, attempting the easier ones first and then moving on to tricks requiring more skill, more speed, more air, more balance, and more confidence. As Rick Thorne said, go out and ride, have fun, but don't pressure yourself.

There is no need for young riders to specialize in any one kind of riding. If a rider likes jumping, that doesn't mean he has to concentrate on vert or dirt. Trying a little of everything at the beginning will make you a better rider. In fact, some basic flatland maneuvers will help any rider with control and confidence if he decides to move on to vert or another discipline. And there are times when a group of riders will have the most fun riding street-style, dealing with natural obstacles and hills.

Some riders may already be able to do some of the tricks discussed in this chapter. Others may read about them for the first time. Reading, however, may not be enough. It's always best to watch someone do a trick or talk with an experienced rider. He can give you invaluable tips. These are just starting points for young riders discovering how much fun they can have on their BMX bikes.

## Flatland Tricks

Flatland tricks are done on a flat surface—no hills, jumps, or obstacles. Some involve more speed than others, and while some can be done in a small area, others require the rider to travel a longer distance. The easier ones will make riding more fun; the more difficult tricks will make you a better and more skillful rider. Always go slow, and don't be discouraged if you can't do them on the first try, or even on the tenth. With persistence and practice, you'll get there.

There are several terms all riders should know. Pegs refer to the extension pieces that can be attached to the front and rear hubs, enabling the rider to stand on them during tricks when his feet are off the pedals. Feathering the brakes is a term used when the brake is pulled lightly—not to stop, but to control speed and help maneuver the bike (for example, when a rider wants to lift the rear tire off the ground while standing on the front pegs, he would feather the brakes to get the tire up without stopping). Scruffing is used when a rider pushes on a tire with his foot to control his speed.

Now, on to some basic tricks.

- *Wheelies.* This is a basic trick almost every boy or girl will try very soon after becoming a competent rider. The concept is simple. It is done by riding on the back wheel with the front wheel off the ground. To do a wheelie, the rider moves forward at a good speed and then pulls up on the handlebars to bring the front wheel up off the ground. He continues to pedal and will soon get the knack of riding down the road on the back wheel. A word of advice: Don't pedal too hard or the front may come up too high. If the rider feels he is beginning to flip back, he should hit the rear brake or dismount by bringing his feet off the pedals and sliding off the back of the bike.

- *Endos.* This is almost a reverse wheelie, because the rider is going to bring the rear wheel off the ground. A rider can learn it by riding forward at a slower pace, slamming the front brake only. At the same time, he should push forward with his arms and the rear tire will lift off the ground. Then, let go of the front brake so the bike rolls forward as the rear tire comes down. As soon as the tire comes down, do it again, only pedaling faster. With practice, a rider will be able to do this at a faster speed and can bring the rear tire higher by pushing harder with his arms. Each time a rider tries it he will find himself rolling further before the rear tire comes back to the ground.

- *Manuals.* A manual is a wheelie without peddling. In other words, you bring the front tire off the ground as you would with a wheelie, then coast at a fast pace, keeping the pedals level with the strong leg back. Riders can bend and straighten their knees to keep their balance. The straighter the knees are, the lower the front end will go. The more they are bent, the higher it will come off the ground. As with the preceding tricks, the manual takes practice and good balance, but once a rider masters it, it will become second nature.

- *Manual bar turns.* This trick leads to others that allow you to turn the handlebars with the front wheel off the ground. The rider goes forward at a good pace, then stands and clenches the back (or widest) part of the seat with his knees. He pulls the front wheel up and turns the handlebars just 90 degrees and back again. This is the basic bar turn. The higher the wheel comes off the ground and the longer the rider can keep it in the air, the more he can turn his handlebars.

- *Manual X-ups.* This is the natural next step embellishing a basic bar turn. The rider begins the same way, but when he pulls the front wheel up, he turns his handlebars 180 degrees or more. (X-Up is a street riding term when a handlebar is turned 180 degrees or more.) As with all manual tricks, if you feel you are up too high and might flip, hit the back brake or try to dismount by releasing the pedals and sliding off the seat.

- *½-bar spins.* This is another trick that will prepare a rider for bigger ones. Cruise at a medium pace, clench the widest part of the seat with

your knees, and lean back a bit. Then, reach across with your dominant hand (depending on whether you are right or left-handed), put it
upside down on the opposite grip, and then pull your hand across to
the other side. The handlebars will have spun 180 degrees. Remember,
move your weight back on the seat so the front wheel is touching, but
with little resistance. If the rider stops with the wheel sideways, he
might get tossed over the handbars. This trick takes practice, but the
rider should keep leaning a little further back until he can do it smoothly.

- *Bar spins.* This is a similar trick, but when the rider leans back he is
going to spin the handlebars 360 degrees (a full turn) with his dominant hand. As the bars come around, he should catch them with both
hands. Ride slowly for this one. The rider should not forget to clench
the seat with his knees and lean way back. Once the rider masters this
technique, he can go a little faster and spin the bars hard to make them
go around more than once.

- *Manual bar spins.* If a rider has mastered the basic manual, this one
won't be too tough. This time, the rider must move faster to get the
front wheel off the ground. He should clench the seat with his knees
and keep the pedals level. Once the wheel is off the ground, he can spin
the bars. A good rider can coast along, spinning the bars as he goes.
The one thing to watch out for is to avoid landing with the front wheel
sideways. If that happens, the rider can be thrown over the handlebars.
Done right, it's a great trick to perform and to watch.

- *Frame stands.* This is another balance trick. The rider begins by standing on the top of the frame right in front of the seat-post while riding at
a medium pace. He should then stand on his right foot with his heel
against the front of the seat-post. When a rider has gotten the knack of
balancing, he may confidently let go of the handlebars. When the rider
has finished the frame stand, he jumps back onto his pedals, which
should remain level during the trick.

- *Front-peg pogos.* This is a fun trick. To begin, the rider should be moving fast enough so that he can get a strong endo going. Then he hits the
front brakes with the pedals level, and quickly jump from the pedals to
the front pegs with both feet. Once there, he begins jumping up and
down while pulling on the handlebars, keeping his feet squarely on the
pegs. When he is ready to stop, he should jump back on the pedals.

This one takes practice, and might sound difficult at first, but once a rider gets used to moving from pedals to pegs, it will fall into place quickly.

- *Tailwhips.* This trick might take longer for a beginning rider to master, but it is good for those who want to attempt more complex flatland maneuvers. Because it's not easy to describe, ask an experienced rider to demonstrate it. In essence, the trick starts by the rider moving at a fairly slow pace. He then places the left pedal straight down so he can pull his right leg over the frame to the left side. Next, he must place his right foot just behind the fork so the tire lightly rubs the bottom of the foot. Then, he hits the front brakes, and at the same time jams his foot into the back of the fork so he gets a good endo. As the rear tire comes up off the ground, the rider kicks the frame around with his left foot. Once he is used to doing this, the frame should turn 180 degrees. One way to complete the trick is by moving the handlebars in a circle. Just follow the frame to keep it going. The rider must then catch the frame with his left foot, bring his right foot back to the pedal, and start pedaling again before the back wheel touches the ground. When a rider has mastered a tailwhip, he is well on his way to becoming a good flatland BMXer.

## Street Tricks

The following are a few tricks to get a BMXer started in the art of street riding. Remember, these brief descriptions present only the essence of the trick. Newer riders will get a much better sense of what they have to do by watching a more experienced rider complete it or by viewing a video in which these tricks are performed. Again, make sure you have a full complement of safety equipment in place. And *never* try any of these tricks without a helmet.

- *The bunnyhop.* This trick provides the basic motion to get a rider's bike into the air. As he is moving forward, he must bring up the front wheel, first by pulling up on the handlebars, then pulling forward. To bring the back up, he must pull his legs up and tuck them behind the seat. After first practicing bunnyhops on flat land, it won't be long before a rider can begin to go up on small obstacles, such as curbs.

- *Catching air.* When a rider goes off a hill, ramp, or any other jump, he is catching air. Some riders launch off the top of the ramp but find they don't really get any air. The knack is to pull up on the handlebars at the tip, or top, of the ramp or jump, then level out and land the bike straight, both wheels touching down at the same time. If the landing isn't flat but a downward slope, then the rider has to lean forward to nose-dive the bike somewhat, and land with both wheels at the same time.

- *Ice pick grind.* Riders perform this trick on the street quite often. It's done at fast speed as the rider approaches a rail or ledge. First, he must bunnyhop and lean back, then land on the ledge or rail with the back peg. Next he slides, or grinds, along the ledge for a bit, then pulls off. It can sometimes help to cake the ledge with wax so the rider won't hit a rough spot and flip over the handlebars.

- *Stair walk.* This trick can be done in slow motion with careful use of the brakes. The rider should begin with a small set of stairs, say four or five. He rides slowly toward the top step and then does a small endo. Next, he moves the front wheel over the step and down to the next one. When the back tire hits the step below it, he should hold the back brake and pull up on the handlebars. He then moves the bike onto the next step and repeats the move until he is at the bottom.

- *Crooked grind.* This is a tough one, which takes perfect timing and placement of the bike. A rider should be prepared to fall more than once as he practices this trick. To do the crooked grind, the rider should approach a low rail or ledge at a slight angle. He must bunnyhop onto it, making sure he lands with the front right peg and rear left peg on the rail. Always try to land the back peg first. The rider should then grind for as long as he can and get off by pulling up on the handlebars and bringing the front wheel over the rail and down. The back wheel will follow.

These are all basic jump, ride, and grind tricks that will help you learn streetstyle riding. Creative riders will invent their own tricks, or variations of those above, as they ride on and over natural obstacles on the street. Master-

**Allen Cooke in action, showing the extension ice pick, done after coming out of the pipe.** Photo by Shawn Frederick

ing a combination of flatland and street tricks will make anyone a fine rider. Riders must remember not to try things that are beyond their abilities. They should learn slowly, ride as much as they can, and practice tricks with friends. There is nothing like competition among friends to bring out the best in riders.

## Vert and Dirt Tricks

These are some of the tricks riders must learn if they want to ride the half-pipe or go off dirt jumps. They involve catching air and being able to control the bike, landing it squarely and safely once tricks are done. Once again, be careful practicing these. Start small. Don't go off huge jumps or try tricks you aren't ready for. Remember, the following are brief descriptions to convey the essence of the tricks. Again, it's always better to see a trick done live or on video, and to ask a veteran rider to offer tips on how to make it easier. As always, Safety First should be your motto.

- *X-up*. This is a simple in-air maneuver, often done for style and looks. Once the rider leaves the jump and is in the air, but before the bike levels out, he should turn the handlebars into a crossed position (sideways). He must, however, be sure there is time to bring the handlebars back to the normal position before he lands.
- *Barspin*. This is similar to the barspin performed on the ground. Once leaving the jump, the rider levels out the bike and clenches the back of the seat with his knees. He must then spin the handlebars with one hand and catch them with the other. Depending on how high the rider ascends, he might even spin them more than once, but he must make sure he is in control of the bars before he dives the bike to land.
- *Superman*. This one shouldn't be too difficult to learn, once a rider can catch enough air and has confidence in his landing. As he leaves the jump, he slides his feet off the back of the pedals and extends them as far out behind him as he can. When bringing his feet back, he must keep his eyes on the pedals so he doesn't miss them, and prepare for the landing.

- *The 360.* A rider might want to begin with a 180, landing the bike backwards, until he gets the knack of spinning. The technique is the same. As he leaves the jump, he should turn the handlebars in the direction he wants to spin, then throw his hips in that direction, as well. The motion should be firm and smooth, not "yanked." As the rider is spinning, he must keep looking for the landing. Don't let it come as a surprise. This one takes control and practice. Riders may wipe out a few times, so they should make sure their safety gear is in place.

- *No-footed can-can.* Again, this is a trick requiring practice but it will give a rider a good idea of how to control his body and bike while in the air. As the rider comes off the jump, he should kick his legs down in order to move the entire bike downward a bit. This will enable him to throw one leg over the top tube so that both of his legs are on the same side of the bike. The rider can then extend his outside leg out as far as he can before bringing it back and swinging the other leg over the tube so that he is set to land. Of course, riders who attempt tricks like this must go off bigger ramps with more speed, so that they catch enough air to give them the time necessary to complete the trick.

- *Front end soaring eagle.* This is another in-air maneuver that will prepare a competent rider for bigger and better tricks. Riders shouldn't try this one unless they have the confidence and ability to control their bikes in midair. The rider must start by heading up the ramp at high speed because he needs to catch a lot of air. Once in the air, he should take his feet from the pedals and place them on the back pegs. At the same time, he should pull up slightly on the handlebars so that the front of the bike is raised slightly. Then comes the spectacular part of the trick: the rider lets go of the handlebars and spreads his arms out like a bird. He must make sure he grabs the handlebars before he transfers his feet from the pegs to the pedals for the landing.

There you have it—a series of tricks which exemplify all the disciplines of freestyle riding. It's merely a beginning for someone who is serious about BMX, but it opens up possibilities and shows how different freestyle is from racing. Freestyle BMXing has brought a whole new approach to riding as well as a new group of riders to the sport. This style of BMX riding has lagged behind some of the other alternative sports in terms of growth, but with increasing television coverage and top riders becoming stars in their own right, more kids are looking at BMX in a different light. For them, it's difficult to get on the bike *without* doing some tricks. Doing tricks is what it's all about.

# 14

# The Amazing Pros and a Bright Future

The tricks outlined in the previous chapter only scratch the surface of what today's stars are doing on their bikes. The pros keep improving, doing more complex maneuvers, and looking to go higher and farther. BMX is a sport where the excitement builds as young riders appear on the scene to challenge the top guys. Rick Thorne says that although more and more young stars are rising, older riders are hanging in there, too. Why not? All these guys can ride and they're all good.

"Some kids are good enough to compete at eighteen and nineteen," he said. "But I don't let numbers mess with my head. It doesn't matter how old you are. At thirty-three, I'm as good as ever, still train hard, and stay focused."

One of Thorne's signature tricks is called the backflip fakie. "Not many do it," he says. "I start on a vert ramp, a 13-foot half-pipe, then take off at the coping and lean back to go into a backward somersault. I flip the bike completely around and then roll down backwards. It's a tough trick. You're going end over end, yet you have to spot the landing and pump out of it. If you land wrong, you can get hurt."

Thorne says that riders today are linking more tricks together. He offered an example: "I know a guy who does a back flip and a tail whip together as one trick. A lot of that comes from the street, where the hardcore riders are linking tricks. That's what I mean by the two factions learning from each other—the hard-cores and the mainstreams."

**Rick Thorne's ramp transfer backflip is caught in this sequence.**
Photo by Shawn Frederick

T. J. Lavin also has some signature tricks that he performs from dirt ramps, his specialty. A sensational-looking maneuver he calls the Superman seat grab is often seen in freestyle motocross, as well, but in motocross the bikes are higher, with more air time. Lavin has to do it quickly before his bike comes down. "You get as much air as you can, then take your feet off the pedals, your hands off the handlebars, and grab the seat as you slide off," he explained. "With your legs behind, you push the seat down so you are completely off the bike, holding onto the seat with only your hands. Then, you have to pull the seat back to you, get on, bring your legs down, and get your hands back on the bars before you land. The trick can also be done with one hand on the seat and one on the handlebars."

Today's riders are also creating some variations on established tricks. "Many tricks are now being done the opposite way," Lavin explained. "In other words, a regular spin is usually done clockwise, but more riders are doing it now counterclockwise. A lot is going on today—older tricks are changing, the top riders keep getting better—making BMX a catch-up game for those who want to reach the top."

## X-Games Performances

Vert, dirt, and flatland BMX freestyle riding have all become popular and exciting competitions at the X-Games. At the 2002 X-Games, held in Philadelphia, Dave Mirra showed he's still the main man when it came to vert. There were two runs for each competitor, the higher score of the two counted toward the medal. Mirra's first run was exceptionally strong and proved to be the best score of the competition. Although Mirra does everything with big air and his own special style, many of his tricks are similar to those described in the previous chapter.

When Mirra dropped into the pipe, he started his run with a no-footed can-can and an X-Up. From that point, he did a big 540 (a 360 plus 180) and then a double whip from the 540. Next came a manual, which set up an opposite flair and another tailwhip. Still riding smoothly, he did a quick one-hander, one-footer, followed those with a big no-hander, and finished with a one-handed ice pick grind across 20 feet of coping. His run featured very difficult tricks performed back-to-back with a fluent style. His score was 94.90

(maximum score 100) and while his second run wasn't quite as solid, his first was enough to get him the gold medal.

Mat Hoffman, known as the Condor, was considered perhaps the biggest threat to Mirra. Those in the sport say that Hoffman, a thirty-year-old Oklahoman, has invented more tricks (and has broken more bones) than any other rider. He holds the world record for the highest air and has done a 900 on his bike. Hoffman continues to compete today despite the many injuries he's suffered over the years. No wonder he's always a threat.

"My whole life I have witnessed many riders retire because of their injuries," Hoffman said. "When the day comes that I choose not to ride anymore, it won't be because of injury. It will be because the challenge of injury will have become more than what my will and determination can overcome. I truly believe that you can do anything you want as long as you are willing

**A vert ramp tailwhip, as demonstrated in this sequence by Rick Thorne.**
Photo by Shawn Frederick

and able to face whatever challenge is presented to you. And I believe you can succeed at anything as long as your ability to face these challenges is what success means to you."

Hoffman's opening trick was a huge no-hander, followed by a double-peg grab, a behind-the-back no-hander and a big, no-footed can-can. Then he went into a lookback 540 to a flair, but his technique faltered as the bike slid out a little, which cost him points. His score was 88.80.

In his second run, Hoffman really went for it, illustrating the competitive nature of the sport. He started with a no-hander, and then did a perfect no-handed 900 that made the crowd roar. This was followed by a 540 no-hander

**Rick Thorne again, this time doing the wall ride.** Photo by Shawn Frederick

and a flair. Again there was a technical slip—Hoffman's handlebars weren't where they were supposed to be. He finished with a 540, a flair, a whip, and a 540 under coping—all in all a magnificent run, but the slight technical slip cost him and his score was 91.40, winning Hoffman the silver medal. This great competition showed how precise champion riders must be, and how judges watch every aspect of each trick.

The X-Games represent the best of the best, and with the BMX vert competition, the sport has reached the same degree of accomplishment as snowboarding, skateboarding, and in-line skating. Its athletes have become more skilled, extremely daring, and have set a standard for more young riders' aspirations. There is little doubt that this form of BMX riding will continue to grow in coming years.

## Dirt Action

While the vert title is decided by the best single run, the gold medal in dirt riding is decided by the riders' average score over four runs, with the lowest score of the four dropped. At the 2000 X-Games, T. J. Lavin came in as one of the favorites. He was up against Allen Cooke and Ryan Nyquist, two other giants of the sport, and the contest was close all the way. In his third run, T. J. was primed to medal or to win. He hit a 360 lookback and a tailwhip, then a barspin and another barspin. Then, he pulled off a superman seat grab 360 that had the crowd cheering. His score of 90.80 was the second best of the competition thus far and placed him in a great spot for the final run.

In his final run, T. J. did what most great riders do. He performed his strongest tricks and tried to do each one a little better than he had ever done them before. He seemed poised to win, with an X-Up 360, a barspin to X-Up, then a tailwhip. Looking to really make a spectacular finish, T. J. tried a huge double-loop to face, but he lost control of the bike, something all riders dread. Neither of the wheels hit squarely on landing, and T. J. crashed. He was knocked cold for several minutes, and the crowd suddenly grew silent. Showing the toughness all riders must have, he got up slowly and walked off.

The wipe-out negated his score for that run, but it was only a brilliant final run by Chris Doyle (91.00) that wrested third place from T. J., who finished fourth. Cooke won gold, with Nyquist second.

Lavin's fall was reminiscent of a remark Lavin made about the nature of dirt riding today: riders have to progress or be left behind. The road to progress, he says, may be "out of control . . . but it sure is fun."

Bronze medal winner Doyle also proved you don't have to be a little guy to ride a 20-inch bike. Standing 6'3", he is one of the tallest riders on the circuit. Considered a style rider, Doyle prefers to forego the more spectacular-looking tricks in favor of those he does to perfection. He admits there are some tricks he doesn't try in competition.

"I don't do backflips in contests," he said. "I can do them, but I don't like them that much. It's not me. I'd rather see someone do a 360 instead of a backflip any day. I think it has a lot to do with where I grew up. In Pennsylvania, we're more focused on style than on big gnarly stuff like that."

Doyle is another BMXer who simply loves to ride. Like many others in the sport, the important thing is being on a bike and doing a lot of everything. Growing up in a state where there are woods and fields, he loves riding various trails, trying new things as he comes across natural changes in the land and an assortment of obstacles. He has become a highly-ranked dirt jumper, but that is almost secondary to his overall love of the sport and the desire to spend as much time on his bike as he can.

# Flatland

Flatland competition is very technical. This version of BMX doesn't normally elicit the oooohs and aaaahs of vert or dirt, because the bikes move in a relatively small area, with the rider doing acrobatic tricks while the bike moves slowly or sometimes not at all. Many of the tricks are variations of the basic flatland tricks described previously. Flatland has sometimes been compared to a gymnastics-type competition. Riders use their bikes in almost the same way gymnasts use a horse or parallel bars, except that the bike moves. The flatland X-Games champion for two years in a row (1999 and 2000) was Martti Kuoppa of Finland.

Kuoppa is considered both an innovator in his sport and a consistently smooth rider who has come to dominate flatland riding. "It actually felt bet-

**Rick Thorne flies high to show his talent while doing the one-foot knack.**
Photo by Shawn Frederick

ter when I won the second time," Kuoppa said, after his victory, "because it made me feel sure that I deserved what I got the year before." Like all top riders, Kuoppa is highly competitive and always trying to top what he has done before. As a Finn, he exemplifies BMX's international appeal.

No matter what aspect of BMX a rider decides to pursue, he will now have plenty of company. T. J. Lavin sees tremendous interest in the sport among riders as young as seven or eight years old. Even some five-year-olds are beginning to veer toward the freestyle side of the sport.

"I see young athletes doing wheelies out of bowls at skateparks all the time now," Lavin said. "They watch videos and see us ride in person, and they want to do such things right away."

Rick Thorne agrees with Lavin. "More and more younger riders will get involved if they look up to the top guys seen on television and want to be like them," he said. "Watching the pros on TV motivates youngsters to ride. Many kids have bikes and boards. Motocross dirt bikes are very expensive, so skateboards and BMX allow youngsters to ride more easily and affordably."

Thorne sees himself as a spokesperson for his sport and because of that, his image is very important to him.

"The next generation looks up to us. They see us in magazines and on TV. I have the respect of young riders and that makes me feel good. Since my goal is to help people do something positive with their lives, to know I have an impact on ten or fifteen year olds tells me I'm doing my job. I'm flattered that these riders hold me in such high regard. The good in these sports, and what you can get from them, go far beyond the X-Games and money."

# PART FOUR

# IN-LINE SKATING

# 15

# A Brief History

For many, in-line skating is purely a recreational activity, a healthful and fun way to skate, get some exercise, and enjoy the outdoors. Young and old alike love putting on the single-line-wheeled skates and taking to the streets, sidewalks, boardwalks, and other places where they can enjoy moving along at any pace they choose. An estimated 30 million people in the United States do in-line skating, making it one of the most popular sports in the country.

A relatively small group, however, follows a more dangerous and exciting form of the sport called aggressive in-line skating, "aggro" for short. These skaters go into the half-pipe and skate ramps with the same verve, skill, and style as in other alternative action sports, and the very best of them compete in the X-Games and Gravity Games, doing some extraordinarily acrobatic tricks—spins and flips—while soaring high in the air. Another contingent still skates the streets the same way skateboarders do, jumping obstacles, grinding down rails and over benches, and showing deft body control on their skates. Because trends and styles can change quickly in any of these sports, many anticipate a boom in aggressive in-line skating soon.

In-line skating has been around, in one form or another, for some 300 years. In the early 1700s, Dutchmen tried to simulate ice skating during the summer months by nailing wooden spools to strips of wood and attaching them to their shoes. The first patented skates, registered in Paris in 1819, were in-line skates, because they featured a single row of wheels, the definition, in effect, of an in-line skate. Until 1863, when James Plimpton invented a skate with four wheels in a rectangular arrangement—two wheels near the toe, two near the heel—all skates had a single line of wheels.

Soon after rectangular, or "quad," skates were invented, the double-alignment of four wheels became the dominant style and roller-skating became a popular recreational activity and later a competitive sport. Jimi Scott, the champion snowboarder, roller-skated long before in-line skates appeared on the market.

"You could see vert roller-skating in skateboard parks in the early 1980s," Scott recalled. "People did some amazing things on the old roller skates back then."

In an early attempt to introduce an in-line skate to consumers, the Chicago Roller Skate Company created in 1966 a boot skate with four in-line wheels. The design, which looks strange today, had the front and rear wheels extend beyond the boot. The style never took off because the skates didn't work very well, and roller-skating remained unchanged until 1980. A pair of hockey-playing brothers, Brennan and Scott Olson of Minneapolis, discovered the Chicago skate boots while looking at used equipment in a sporting goods store.

The discovery sparked an idea. The Olsons realized that the single line of wheels attached to the skate's boot resembled an ice skate. If they could create a better single-line skate, they would have a way to practice hockey when no ice was available. Soon they had developed such an in-line skate using hockey boots, polyurethane wheels, and rubber heel brakes. They began making more of them and selling them to their friends. A short time later they formed a company called Rollerblade to manufacture and market the skates. In 1984 they sold the company to a group able to market the skates nationally, and within five years there were more than 3 million total skaters in the country.

At that time, in-line skating was so closely associated with one company and one skate that the sport was universally called "rollerblading." Now it's called in-line skating and, at the start of the twenty-first century, statistics indicate that in-line skating is the fifth largest participatory sport overall and the number one participatory sport among boys ages six to seventeen.

It isn't surprising that a few young skaters would be tempted to try new and daring maneuvers. This aspect of the sport, which would later become known as aggro, had its roots in skateboarding. In 1981, skaters A. J. Jackson, Pat Parnell, Doug Boyce, Chris Morris, and others began riding their in-line skates on the same types of streets and vert terrains used in skateboarding. As relatively few in-line skaters were performing tricks and stunts, and since the sport as a whole didn't boom until the late 1980s and early 1990s, such skaters were still something of a novelty.

Jon Julio was among the second generation of in-line skaters. Born in San Jose, California, in 1977, Jon loved basketball, music, break dancing and, eventually, disk-jockeying. Unlike some of the other athletes profiled in this book, he had nothing against traditional team sports. In fact, Julio said that he always had a "passion" for basketball. But he found something he liked more.

Around the age of sixteen, he and his friends watched a video called *Airborne*, which featured in-line skaters doing tricks and stunts. They were soon watching other videos and began copying the things they had seen.

"Arlo Eisenberg and Chris Edwards were, to me, the two fathers of the sport," Julio explained. "They were the first to do a lot of the street tricks. In *Airborne*, Chris Edwards rode ramps, grinded over rails, jumped obstacles—all of it street skating. Arlo Eisenberg made a video called *The Hoax*, which also featured street skating. These two videos set the standard for the sport then. People still talk about those videos today."

With videos to encourage him, Julio spent more time on his skates and less on the basketball court. "Skating became more personal to me than basketball," Julio said. "You could express your own style and attitude. The fear factor also played into it. I think I liked the element of danger. I think that people in these sports thrive on danger, because there is always some risk when you try new tricks. With skating, the idea of sliding down rails and jumping was new then. The culture was new, the magazines new, and tricks on skates were new, as well.

"We used to skate on the streets most of the time. There were a few skateboard parks in California then, and we went there, too. But we were kicked out of a lot of places. Skateboarders and in-liners were condemned in the same breath then because both were done on the streets. Then, as now, street skating is huge and the main attraction for most in-liners."

What gave the sport a boost was the introduction of a tough in-line skate built to take the aggression and abuse of streetstyle skating: the Rollerblade Lightning TRS skate. This skate, which made its debut in 1988, was more

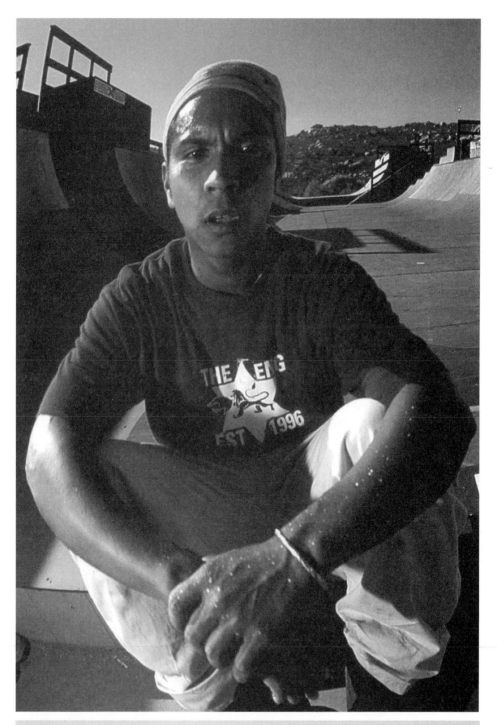

**Aggro in-line skater Jon Julio.** Photo by Jess Dyrenforth

durable than those sold previously. It was the first skate with a nylon reinforced frame and it allowed skaters to grind on the street and vert ramps, as well as ride the coping at the top of a ramp with more control. Chris Edwards quickly began using the new skates to jump on stair railings and grind his way down.

Soon, the first small in-line skating contests began to appear. In 1994, Mark Shays, Mark Billik, and Rick Start founded the first-ever national skate competition tour. A year later, ESPN inaugurated X-Games, which helped put aggressive in-line skating—vert and streetstyle—on the map. Sponsors and contracts for pro skaters soon followed, and in 1996, aggressive skating, skateboarding, and BMX freestyle were combined for a multi-sport nationwide tour. The sports were soon selected to be featured in the closing ceremonies of the 1996 summer Olympics.

However, such popular acceptance didn't mean that aggressive in-line skating would follow the same path as the other alternative sports. "For some reason, about 1998 or 1999, sales of skates went down and the sport seemed to lose some of its appeal," said Jon Julio, who has skated during both good and bad times. "A lot of the pros were barely getting by."

The growth of skateboarding, snowboarding, and BMX biking held more appeal than in-line skating for many young athletes, who found a greater challenge in these other sports. If an athlete wanted to compete in an action sport, generally he chose one of the other three over in-line. Fans, too, seemed to be attracted more to skateboarding and BMX. Why this preference developed is the subject of much conjecture. Did some athletes feel that in-line skating, even in vert and street, was less difficult than other action sports and thus not as great a challenge? Considering the mind-boggling aerial stunts today's aggro skaters perform while flying out of the half-pipe, the appeal is still very much alive.

Other forms of skating continue to be popular. The International Inline Skating Association (IISA) was formed in 1991 to promote the sport, to develop educational programs about safe skating, and to certify instructors. IISA does not organize or sanction competitions, but encourages more people to skate, ensuring that the sport will thrive on a recreational level. Competitions were held in speed skating, artistic or figure skating (which emulates figure skating on ice), and roller hockey. Roller hockey itself became popular, its players forming leagues.

The aggressive form of the sport began to rebound, thanks to the hard-core kids who hung in there in spite of having fewer sponsors or competition venues as those in other sports

"When things didn't look good for our sport, we came up with our own products and produced videos, as well as our own events," Jon Julio said. "I organized an event called IMYTA, which stood for the I Match Your Trick Association. The concept was like HORSE in basketball. You do a trick and the others have to match it. If they miss, they get a letter. I-M-Y-T-A. The winner is the last guy left in. We started with some forty entrants, and would work our way down to four finalists. Usually, the contests were held where there were natural obstacles like ledges, big rails, and drop-offs."

Julio, who has won the world championship of the National In-Line Skate Series, has seen the ages of pros rise in recent years. "At the beginning pros were fifteen and sixteen. Now the pros are in their early twenties and also get involved in producing graphic design, art, and videos to create an industry."

Currently, there are two main events in aggro competition: street style and vert (the half-pipe). In street competition, skaters perform tricks while jumping over boxes, ramps, and rails on a streetlike surface. In vert a sixty-second routine of tricks and stunts is performed in a half-pipe, similar to those used in skateboarding, snowboarding, and BMX. The Aggressive Skaters Association (AGA) is now the major organizing and sanctioning body of the sport, managing in-line skating events at the X-Games and Gravity Games, and conducting a world championship. There is also an amateur circuit which comprises some fifty events in more than twenty countries.

The sport has gained an international flavor, as outstanding skaters from such countries as Japan and Australia have taken their place among the best in the world. With the increased popularity of aggro, more young competitors are joining the sport sooner, lowering the age of the top skaters again to the middle and upper teens.

Although Aggressive In-Line Skating appears ready to take its place alongside the radical factions of snowboarding, skateboarding, and BMX-ing, keep in mind that in-line skating is a sport for everyone, which millions of people pursue for fun and relaxation.

# 16

# Let's Go Skating

Each year, more people put on in-line skates for the first time. The reasons people skate are as different as the ages of the beginners. The sport offers something for everyone, even senior citizens. When starting out, however, it is necessary for a newcomer to select the type of skating he or she wants to do. As with the other sports discussed in this book, an in-line skater should purchase the right equipment. As well as skates tailored for men or women, skates are made for recreational skating, for aggressive, for speed skating, for roller hockey. Bear in mind, however, that a skater can begin with one type of skate and switch to another if his skills improve or he decides to try a new style. The differences in the skates are as follows.

- *Recreational.* Although these skates are designed for leisurely glides around the neighborhood or on a boardwalk, they can also be used when skating for fitness. Comfort and durability are priorities and skates usually are made with a hard outer frame and a soft or hard boot. Recreational skates are typically equipped with four wheels with a wheel size ranging between 70 and 80 mm.
- *Aggressive.* Not surprisingly, these skates are designed for jumping, rail riding, and half-pipe action. They are very solid and sturdy, with smaller, hard wheels to provide maneuverability and durability. The

skates can be fitted with special modifications to allow skaters to ride rails and ramps.

- *Speed.* These are lighter and less robust skates than either the recreational or aggressive models. They are designed strictly for fast skating and have longer frames, with a fifth wheel added for more stability and longer strides. The larger wheels on these skates allow for greater acceleration, and there is no braking system.

- *Hockey.* Hockey skates are similar in style and construction to traditional ice hockey skates. They are very durable, with leather uppers and significant padding for protection, and often they have a lace-up closure system and smaller wheels for enhanced turning ability. Some skates have large wheels in the back and smaller wheels in front for even better turning power. They also have no braking system.

- *Women's.* Skates designed for women offer a wider forefoot, narrower heel, and high instep. They are also cut lower in the back to accommodate a woman's calf.

Wheels are usually made of polyurethane, a molded compound which lends itself to different thicknesses and wheel hardness. Typical in-line skate wheels are 70–80 mm in diameter, larger wheels designed for speed, smaller for maneuverability. Recreational skates usually come with 70–72 mm wheels to provide a low, stable center of gravity. Midsize wheels are 72–76 mm, while higher grade skates come with wheels up to 80 mm to allow for faster skating.

Hockey wheels tend to be smaller, for maneuverability, and are more tapered than other wheels, for better stability in a turn. Aggressive skate wheels are very small (55–67 mm) and are best for stunt riders. These wheels are manufactured to be very hard, in order to withstand the grinding and jumping done in freestyle stunts. Racing wheels are larger (78–80 mm) and are the thinnest of all wheels, as they are made for more speed and less stability.

It's important that skaters rotate their wheels in order to avoid excessive or uneven wear. This should be done at least once a week by regular skaters and after each use by very aggressive skaters. Wheels should be changed when they show excessive wear on all sides. It's unsafe to skate with worn wheels.

The frames hold the skate's components in place. For the most part, recreational frames are fabricated from aluminum alloy or nylon and fiberglass composites. Always be sure the frames you select are designed for the type of skating you plan to do. Metal frames are stiffer, faster, and lighter, and cost more.

The hard shell of the boot is made of molded plastic and is similar to a ski boot. The lower half covers and protects the foot, while the upper half wraps around and supports the ankle. The two halves are connected with a hinge system which allows the ankle and boot to flex forward naturally. There is also a soft boot made with an external plastic cuff to provide support, like a hiking boot. These boots are very breathable and lightweight, and are generally secured by laces. Shoes without laces will have buckles that snap closed and are the quickest to put on and take off.

Wheel bearings are rated for quality. There are two kinds, serviceable and non-serviceable. The serviceable bearings have a metal shield with a removable "C" ring, which is a removable shield made of plastic or rubber. These may be taken apart to be cleaned, lubricated, or replaced. Nonserviceable bearings have a metal shield that protects them. They need only be wiped with a clean cloth.

The most common form of braking system is a pad or cylinder on the rear wheel, which stops movement by applying pressure on the heel. Most brake pads have what is called a wear line, to show how much life remains in the brake. The brake should be replaced before this wear line is reached.

It's important to have a thorough knowledge of in-line skates and equipment, because you should always have the right style of skate, of the best quality you can afford. There is also a safety factor. Even if you don't skate aggressively, you can be hurt. The better the equipment and the more you know about safety, the better are your chances that skating will be a rewarding experience.

An estimated 90,000 moderate-to-serious in-line skating injuries occur each year—a sobering statistic. Fractures and head injuries are not uncommon, and many injuries are sustained by skaters under the age of fifteen. As early as August 1991, the U. S. Consumer Product Safety Commission (CPSC) issued a formal "Safety Alert" as a warning to consumers, cautioning them that "in-line roller skating—a popular new sport—can be hazardous if skaters do not wear helmets and other protective equipment or do not learn to skate and stop safely."

The CPSC's recommendations still apply to skaters today, especially recreational skaters who may not possess the skills of aggressive skaters. Their rules of safety are as follows:

- Always wear a helmet, one that is intended for either skateboarding or in-line skating. In addition, skaters should wear knee and elbow pads, as well as gloves that include a wrist guard. The wrist guard can go a long way to prevent fractures when a skater tries to break a fall with his or her hands.
- Always skate on smooth, paved surfaces without any vehicular traffic. Avoid skating on streets, driveways, or surfaces with water, sand, gravel, or dirt.
- Learn to stop safely, using the brake pads at the heel of most in-line skates.
- Do not skate at night because of the difficulty in being seen and the difficulty seeing obstacles or other skaters.

According to the CPSC, most injuries are caused by skaters not knowing how to stop or turn properly, by skating too fast without control, by skating on rough or uneven pavement, gravel or sand, or by engaging in other high-risk behaviors.

Freestyle and aggressive skaters in the half-pipe take more chances and risk greater injury than recreational skaters. However, even the most aggressive of skaters should wear helmets, as well as knee and elbow pads, and gloves. The type of skating a person pursues is entirely up to them, but everyone should remember: Safety first.

## A Few More Basics

The easiest part of in-line skating is moving forward. Skaters quickly learn to turn their foot out at an angle and push off, the same as ice skaters. With a little practice they are pushing one foot after the other and skating.

Controlling their skates is another thing. That's why stopping is so important, especially when skaters begin to increase their skating speed. Using the
brake pad is obviously the first and often the best way to stop, and for a variety of reasons. Here are six:

1. A skater can use the brake pad to stop, even at very high speeds.
2. The brake pad allows skaters to keep both skates on the ground while
   stopping, which helps them keep their balance.
3. Stopping with the brake pad allows the skater to maintain a narrow
   profile. In other words, it lets him stop in a straight line.
4. A skater can still steer while using the pad.
5. The sound made by the brake pad will alert others to the skater's pres-
   ence.
6. The brake pad is also the most cost-effective way to stop over and over
   again. Other stopping methods will wear out the wheels much more
   quickly, and wheels are considerably more expensive to replace than
   the brake pad.

The easiest way to learn how to use the brake pad is for the skater to
begin coasting with his skates a shoulder-width apart. As he coasts, he
should scissor his feet back and forth a few times to get used to the weight
shift. In other words, put one foot in front of the other. When the skater is
ready to apply the brake, he should again scissor his feet so that the braking
skate is out in front. The skater should then lift the toe of his brake skate and
press the surface with the heel. He should keep his body weight-centered and
even slightly on his back skate while learning the technique. The key to balance is a straight back and bent knees.

The more pressure a skater puts on the brake pad the faster he will stop.
This allows him to stop even at high speeds. To get maximum stopping
power a skater should put his entire body weight onto the brake by lifting
his back foot, and leaning onto the brake. He should always keep one wheel
of the brake skate on the ground when he leans back on the brake because
he may need that single wheel to serve as a pivot. Using this method, it is
possible to stop within fifteen to twenty feet even when skating at more than
twenty miles per hour.

A skater can steer while braking by keeping the brake pad on the ground and pivoting slightly on the heel wheel, to take him in the direction he wants. This can be useful when skating down a narrow and curvy path or while trying to avoid a curb, a pedestrian, or any other obstacle. Be aware that a half-worn brake pad provides better leverage than either a new brake or a worn-out brake. Some skaters will saw off part of the bottom of new brakes to avoid the breaking-in period. New skaters who want to do this should let an experienced skater show them how to do this, so they don't damage the pad and render it less effective. The pad must be cut evenly and at the same angle as it originally sat on the skate.

The use of the brake pad is the first method a new skater should learn, but there are some other ways for skaters to stop For example, a slow-moving skater can use the V-Stop or Snowplow method. This involves pointing the heels inward if skating backwards, or pointing the toes together while going forward, and allowing the skates to bang into each other. Skaters should always be prepared to lean forward or backward, because this shift may direct their body in the direction they want to go. How much lean depends on the speed of the skater.

At slow speeds, beginners can also stop by using a runout, which means skating from a faster surface to a slower one. In other words, if a skater is on a packed dirt path or a concrete walk, he can skate off to a grass area (if one is available) and this will reduce his speed. It is also possible to skate into a stationary object, such as a wall, and to absorb the impact with the arms. Skaters should only use this method at slow speeds, using their arms as cushioning springs and turning their heads to the side to avoid a frontal impact.

Advanced skaters will learn other ways to stop. One good technique at higher speeds is the chop stop, which is similar to the way many ice skaters stop. It is done by turning both skates and hips perpendicular to the direction of travel. The skates should be at an angle, so that the skater can push the edge of the wheels against the ground. To maintain balance, the skater should keep one skate mainly beneath his body while the other is placed forward to stop him. Most of the scraping or shredding is done by the lead skate, where the inside of the lead leg makes a sharp angle against the ground.

These are maneuvers all skaters learn as they progress in the sport. They will observe other skaters doing them, see them in videos, and ideally someone will demonstrate them personally. It never hurts to have an experienced skater as a coach, even for a short time.

## A Word About Falling

Everybody falls, sooner or later. Aggressive skaters can crash. Surprisingly, there are times when falling might be the practical thing to do. Though it should be used as a last resort, every skater should know a few things about taking a fall. Falling can be practiced at low speeds. In many cases, if a skater lands on his safety equipment—knee and elbow pads—he will walk away in good shape.

If a skater moving at a relatively slow speed feels he has to fall in order to stop, the way to do it is to collapse the body so that the primary scraping areas are the knee pads and gloves with wrist guards. To do it, skaters should bend at the knees, and fall first on their knee pads, and then on their wrist guards. Always keep the wrists loose since the risk of an injury may be still present. If a skater falls backwards, his rear end will serve as a cushion. He can also spread out the shock by using his arms. A word of caution: The tailbone is prone to injury or fracture with any hard fall on the rear, so be careful.

Needless to say, a fall at high speed may be dangerous. Even if a skater collapses onto his protection gear it may not be enough. If he has to fall at high speed, it's best to take the brunt of the fall with the entire body except, of course, the head. A helmet protects only so much. The key to taking this kind of fall is to roll. When a skater is coming down a hill and feels himself falling, he should try to turn sideways, away from the direction of travel, and fall uphill. Upon impact, he should keep his body loose, with hands up near the face or over the head. If the skater rolls quickly, chances are he'll get up and walk away unharmed.

## Skating Downhill

Skating downhill may be the first step in becoming more than just a recreational skater. It may even be your daring first step toward becoming a streetstyle or vert aggro skater. Of course, any skater might find himself coming down a hill at one time or another, but those looking for an added touch of excitement are the ones who will seek out the hills and say, *I can do this.*

Downhill skating should not be on the agenda for week one of anyone's skating career. It should be attempted only after a skater has mastered the basic skills—turning, braking, and good balance. This means knowing several alternative stopping methods besides the brake pad, and having firm control over your skates. No skater wants to take a bad spill while going twenty-five or thirty miles per hour. The following are a few things to consider before a skater challenges a major hill.

- Never be without any of the safety gear (helmet, pads) when riding hills.
- Check out a hill before skating it. If a skater hits a pothole at twenty-five miles an hour, all the skating skills in the world might not help him.
- Always have safety in mind. If a skater is going down a public hill, he must know the traffic patterns, road signs, stop lights, intersections, and pedestrian crossings. If he feels it's too dangerous, he should not skate it. If he does, he must always make sure he can get out of harm's way quickly.
- Skaters should practice using their brake pads at high speed so that stopping becomes second nature to them.
- Start riding a hill in sections. The first time on the hill, the skater should start half or a quarter of the way from the bottom. Once he has done that, he can work his way up a little higher until he feels he is ready to ride the entire hill.
- A skater should control his speed by braking every five to ten yards. This is almost like pumping the brakes on a car. If a skater rolls freely, he may suddenly find himself moving at a rate of speed at which he is not comfortable or, in some cases, he may careen out of control.
- Skaters should always keep their bodies relaxed. If they are tense while riding a hill, even the slightest bump or pothole can cause them to wipe out.

Keeping these rules in mind, all one needs is practice. By mastering downhill skating, anyone can become a better overall skater and acquire the confidence and skills needed to pursue other styles of skating.

"All new skaters must learn at their own pace," advised pro skater Jon Julio. "Videos can help, friends can inspire you. Balance remains the key. Both skiing and ice skating can help an in-line skater because of the similarity of motion. But even if you haven't pursued those sports, don't be afraid to put on in-line skates. Repetition and practice will eventually make you a good skater.

Those who aren't interested in the more radical disciplines or aggressive skating can enjoy in-line skating for what it is—an enjoyable, healthful form of recreation. For those who want to do more, read on.

# 17

## Street and Vert

Street and vert, the two disciplines of aggressive in-line skating, are beginning to attract more young skaters every year. Because "aggro" skating has trailed other sports in terms of popularity and exposure, today's top skaters are on a mission, to prove the level of their abilities and the value of their sport. In a field wide open to new skaters, new stars, and more exciting and skillful tricks, aggro is, in the minds of many alternative sports observers, on the brink of breaking out big.

Of the two aggro disciplines, streetstyle is by far the more popular form, though the number of vert skaters is increasing, as well, with vert gaining popularity in the U.S. and abroad, with world-class riders making their mark on the international skating scene.

Though in-line skating has taken longer than skateboarding, snowboarding, and BMX to find its own identity and develop its own culture, it's now well on its way, as Jon Julio explains.

"There has always been a cultural aspect to alternative sports," he said. "Young skaters are involved with music, graphic design, videos, style, and fashion. It can be a lot of fun getting involved in everything that goes with skating, right down to the clothes and logos."

Because alternative sports athletes often dress differently from others, have their own lingo, and listen to music they can call their own, they've been looked upon as different, at best, as outlaws and rebels, at worst. The same applies to hardcore in-liners, where slang terms are byproducts of the subculture. For example, a word like *gnarly*, used to describe a trick that is dangerous and difficult, has always been part of the alternative sports culture. It's the same for *sick*, which in the alternative sports world doesn't mean being ill but describes something considered really cool, whether it be a trick or clothing, a video or music.

Let's take a look at some of the skills needed to make the move to the street and vert disciplines of in-line skating.

## Stairs, Curbs, Walls, and Rails

The ability to ride stairs, curbs, walls, rails and other obstacles is central to the streetstyle side of in-line skating. If that sounds familiar it is because it is very similar to skateboarding and BMX biking, where the same obstacles are fair game. Stairs, for example, weren't intended for in-line skaters to go down them, but skaters do it, and many develop their own techniques. Wide stairs which aren't too steep (wide, referring to the depth of each plank, front to back) are the best kind to ride.

Riding stairs works best when the skater keeps one foot in front of the other. Skaters using this method must remember to keep foot placement constant. They should not fall into the trap of bringing their rear foot up alongside the front foot. It's best to slide the front foot out first and place the trailing knee, bent, almost behind the leading one. That way, the trailing leg will absorb most of the shock. If the skater relaxes, the ride will be much smoother.

Some skaters prefer to go off steps at an angle, turning their lead skate forty-five degrees. This way, they are going down one side to another, instead of straight. However, a variety of techniques can work. Good skaters can go down stairs backwards or jump several stairs at once. This, of course, takes considerable practice and skill. Go slow; no one wants to fall down a flight of stairs. Start small; ride only three or four stairs at a time. Don't try to tackle a staircase of twelve or fifteen steps. It's a longer way to the bottom in a lot of ways.

Here are a few tips for skaters learning to ride stairs:

- Skate at reasonable speed. A skater cannot ride stairs in slow motion. Because many skaters tend to slow down as they descend the stairs, they should begin at a moderate speed and try to maintain it. Experienced, aggressive skaters will often use a wider stance and lean into the slope of the stairs to avoid losing speed. New skaters, however, must be careful. They should not lean forward too much or they might take a quick, unwanted trip to the bottom.
- Be prepared for a bumpy, jarring ride. Some called it stair "bashing," because all riders will bump down stairs to some degree. Some skaters may not like the feeling of riding stairs, even though they find they can do it well.
- Backwards is smoother. Believe it or not, some riders prefer to ride stairs backwards. While this sounds very difficult and dangerous, the ride can be smoother because of the more natural flex of the ankle in the backwards position. While it is a more daunting and intimidating ride at first, some skaters say it's actually easier to ride stairs going backwards. Obviously, this is something a beginning skater should not attempt until he has good overall skating skills and the confidence that goes with them.
- Never, ever, ride a set of stairs without a helmet.

## Curb and Rail Grinds

Curbs and other grinds are a favorite of street skaters. In reality, grinding is a form of sliding. Those who want to do this kind of riding should look into a special skate. "Skates made especially for grinding have a frame lower to the ground, with more space between the two front wheels and two rear wheels," Jon Julio explained. "Some skates have special grinding blocks in the middle between the wheels, made especially to withstand the friction of constant grinding."

While many skaters find curb grinding the easiest form of street skating, it may be easier to begin with a low rail, perhaps four to eight inches above the ground. The rail should be small enough to fit between the second and third wheels, where the grinding block is located. The skater begins by going directly at the rail. Then he should jump slightly and land with his feet spread, with the rail between the second and third wheels. Once he gets the knack of jumping onto the rail, he can begin approaching it from less and less of an angle. Always keep the feet spread. This will lessen the chance of a fall. Before long, the skater will find he can slide sideways along the rail before dismounting.

If skaters decide to grind along a concrete curb, it's best to wax the curb first with paraffin or bar soap. Wax a ten-foot-long portion around the edge of the curb and about three inches wide on top. One type of curb grind is called a "soul" grind. To do it, the skater should stand alongside a curb that is approximately four to eight inches high. Jump onto the curb, with the edge of the curb between the second and third wheel on the front skate and on the outside sole of the back boot. Once a skater does this, he is ready to grind. The skater approaches the curb by skating almost parallel to it, then jumps onto the curb in the position described above, with his weight distributed evenly on both feet. Skaters who find they are having trouble staying on the curb can try looking down at it, which may help them keep their front foot on the curb. They can then grind across for as long as possible.

Many skaters prefer to remove a wheel when doing rail slides. If a wheel is removed, the skater can land in the gap and slide sideways on the rail on the frame of the boot, and have more surface on which to grind. Grinding blocks can be put on the skate in place of the wheel to create a larger gap. Normally, skate parks provide rails on which to practice. Good skaters can do both frontside and backside grinds and slides, and the top street freestylers will even do 180s and 360s while grinding and sliding. It's a big part of the freestyle scene.

Jon Julio has performed a pair of favorite tricks involving grinds. Neither is easy. One is called a fish brain. "It's nicknamed after an old pro skater, Tom Fry," Julio said, "and is a variation of a one-footed grind. You do it on a ledge, going up and grinding on the base of one foot, sliding on the sole of the foot and frame. At the same time, you reach down and grab the side of the skate on your other foot."

Julio calls the second trick the unity grind. "You grind on the boot when your legs are crossed," he said. "Both feet make contact with the object on

**An unidentified streetstyle skater slides down a long handrail with amazing skill.** Photo by Jess Dyrenforth

the boots and side of the frame. It takes practice. All skaters should practice jumping, so they can get up onto the objects and be very comfortable on their skates before trying grinds. You also have to understand falling, and be able to catch yourself."

## Ramps and the Half-Pipe

Freestyle and aggro skaters will need additional skills as they hone their abilities and add more tricks and maneuvers to their repertoire. Skaters should proceed slowly, mastering one skill before moving on to another. Again, the descriptions of the techniques given in this book are not to be considered a complete "how-to." They are designed to provide skaters with an introduction to learning these maneuvers. Watching other skaters live and on video, and seeking instruction from experienced skaters is always best.

Jumping on skates is not the same as jumping with a snowboard, skateboard, or BMX bike. With in-line, skaters jump the same way they would without skates, but they must grow accustomed to doing it on wheels. Skaters can practice the motion of jumping up on an object—even doing 180s and 360s—without their skates on. To jump up or over something, leap from both feet at once, using your arms, knees, and hips to get your lift. With a 180 or 360, power your rotation from your torso and carry your legs around for the ride.

On spins, it also helps to hold the arms out in an L-shape, one to the front and one out to the side, and swing them to start the rotation. Some feel that practicing spins without skates is imperative, because if a person can't do a 360 spin without skates, he will never be able to do it with skates.

Strength and balance are necessary to most kinds of jumps. Jumping without skates might teach you technique, but once the skates are on, balance becomes key. To be able to jump up and over things gives skaters a great edge for some flashy streetstyle skating. To be able to do 180s and even 360s is a supplemental skill for both grinding and jumping. The more skills a skater has, the more fun the sport can be.

# Ramps

Ramps are second nature to aggro skaters, just as they are to snowboarders, skateboarders and BMXers who go into the half-pipe and love to do tricks while catching air. Before riding a ramp, skaters must have a feel for being in the air and be able to land squarely on their skates. Small jumps, even those beginning off a curb and then going a bit higher, will help give the skater confidence. Even with practice, ramps can be daunting. Because of the built-in danger, anyone who wants to learn the art of ramp skating should remember the following rule of thumb.

Skaters should never start from the top of a ramp, even if they want to get the sense of jumping off. Regardless of whether he's using a small ramp, such as a three-foot quarter-pipe, the skater should not start from the top of the ramp until he is able to get there by skating up the transition. Skaters who make it to the top must not stop abruptly. In more than one case, when a young skater stops in such a way, he has fallen backwards and been injured.

# Getting into the Half-Pipe

Riders ought to get used to the transition of going from a flat to a sloped surface. There are two kinds of inclines—a flat ramp or incline, and a curved incline, such as you find in the half-pipe. The curved incline may at first lend a strange sensation to skating, so new skaters have to get used to it. But even with a flat incline, a beginning ramp rider must be able to skate up the incline and go. One way to get used to an incline, especially the curved variety, is to skate up the transition, turn around, and skate down. Skaters should practice this until it becomes a fluid and relaxed maneuver.

Once a skater is comfortable with the transitions, he has to learn how to pump, to gain speed when he is in a pipe or on any kind of incline. Even though a rider is skating at a good clip, once he tries to coast uphill, gravity and friction will slow him down. Pumping isn't easy to explain. Skaters must watch someone doing it to fully understand the technique. As a skater comes up to the transition, he must bend his knees. Once he starts up the incline he must push his feet out, which will bring him to a standing position. Pushing against the incline, he'll find that he has gained speed. Both in-line skaters and skateboarders pump this way. Some don't even realize they are doing it.

Pumping, however, is the secret to ramp and pipe riding. The better a skater can pump, the more speed he will generate and the more air he will catch, enabling him to go higher off the ramp or out of the pipe. By pumping with bad technique or without pumping at all, a skater won't gain speed and won't get high enough to perform complex tricks. In a half-pipe, skaters want to obtain sufficient speed in the transition to grab onto the top of the pipe and pull themselves up on the platform. At this point, they are almost ready to drop in. Some prefer to sit on the edge the first time and slide down, in order to get used to the height and speed of the slide. The next time, a skater might sit on the edge and push himself forward. From there, he can stand up. If he does this a few times he should get used to skating down the pipe. Finally, he is ready to drop in standing up.

New skaters in the pipe must always wear a helmet and a good set of knee pads. And when they drop in, they should make sure to bend their knees or they might find themselves sliding down face first. Once a skater is inside the pipe, he can pump up and down the sides and can begin a few basic maneuvers, such as a 180 at the top and skating back down, and doing a simple fakie, where it goes in the air, but does nothing, not even turning around, just drops back into the pipe but skates down backwards. That isn't as easy as it sounds, and takes a great deal of practice.

No one becomes a vertical skater overnight. Getting into the half-pipe and learning to pump up and down the sides is only the tip of the iceberg. But everyone has to start somewhere and getting used to the pipe is always step one. Watch, learn, get tips, practice, and listen. Pretty soon you'll be able to do some basic tricks and from there you can go as far as you want.

## Launch Ramps

Some skaters prefer to launch themselves off ramps, do a trick in the air, and then land. Others will set up a pair of ramps, launching off one and landing on the other. Some skaters will launch off a flat object, such as the top of a short staircase (four or five stairs), and do a 180 or more before they land. There are many ways skaters can launch and jump, and each one takes practice. Always start small and then work up to something bigger.

Some street skaters will look for low ramps that have been already set up or built into curbs for bikes or wheelchairs, and launch off of them, catching moderate air and jumping on to the sidewalk. Of course, skaters take care they aren't going to slam into an unsuspecting pedestrian.

Many young skaters prefer to build their own launch ramps for the purpose of jumping and landing beyond the ramp. With this, too, always start small. Don't build a huge ramp with a long drop, something you may not be ready for. Using a ramp about eight feet long and two or three feet tall is a good way to start. A skater can hit the ramp at good speed, skate up, and launch. It's also helpful for stability purposes to place a small platform at the top. Homemade ramps made from plywood and two-by-fours will do fine.

Undoubtedly, there is a great deal to learn if you want to be a good street or vert skater. You need skills, courage, and common sense. As Jon Julio has said, many young athletes today want to advance as quickly as possible, but it's important to remember that every skater doesn't have to be as good as his or her favorite professional vert skater, or the latest streetstyle or park champion. As with any of these sports, object number one is to have fun. If having fun means skating leisurely around a track or on the street, that's fine. If it means being able to grind and slide along some rails or curbs, there's nothing wrong with that. And if a skater won't be happy until he is in the air, he should go for it. Just do it all slowly, with some good supervision and a little coaching. Trial and error can sometimes be painful. Watch a skater who is at least a notch or two ahead of you in skill and technique. That's always the best way to learn.

# 18

## Aggro—the Future of In-Line

In today's alternative sports world, in-line skating poses something of a riddle. Consider the following. It's much easier for the average person to learn how to in-line skate recreationally than to skateboard. Snowboarding is more expensive and requires a mountain in a snowy climate. Not everyone wants to ride a BMX bike. For these reasons, recreational in-line skating continues to attract a huge number of riders, young and old, who enjoy a leisurely skate for fun and exercise. Why, when it comes to catching air and the other more difficult disciplines of the sport, have skateboarding, snowboarding, and BMX surged far ahead in popularity? Aggressive in-line skating has not received as much publicity as the others, nor does it have as many participants in the United States. (Currently, many of the world's best skaters are from other countries, such as Japan and Brazil.)

Aggressive in-line skating fits well within the parameters of today's alternative sports. Yet a top pro like Jon Julio admits that as of 1998, sales of skates had slumped and the sport had lost some of its appeal. Many pros were not earning nearly the same amounts of money as their counterparts in other sports. According to Julio, however, hardcore skaters are not giving up. They continue to work toward building an industry on a par with the others.

Part of the problem can perhaps be found in the attitude of many athletes in other alternative sports, who have expressed mixed feelings about aggro

158

in-line skating. Jon Julio has acknowledged that "skateboarding is a bit more difficult because of the board." In other words, skaters don't have to worry about maintaining contact with a board. But does that difference in difficulty extend into the radical aggro world?

Rune Glifberg, a champion skateboarder, who harbors some of those doubts, acknowledges that some astonishing things can be done on skates.

"I grew up with a guy who was a roller skater in Copenhagen," Glifberg said. "He was a gymnast and great on the trampoline, and one of the first guys to do backflips on his skates. He was truly amazing. Had he gone in-line, he probably could have been a champion."

Because even the aggressive skaters have a skate and boot on each foot, Glifberg feels they have an advantage over the skateboarder. "To me, in-line skating doesn't seem very skillful. Skaters don't have to worry about losing the skates. They can make mistakes and still do the trick. From what I've seen, it's a sport where girls are just as good as the boys. That doesn't happen in all sports. It's also a sport that doesn't take long to learn."

One problem, in Rune Glifberg's opinion, is that in-line skating doesn't have much that distinguishes it. "Right now I don't see anything about in-line that makes it special. Skaters copy a little of this and a little of that from skateboarding. They don't seem to have their own direction. Snowboarding adopts things from skateboarding, but boarders have their own disciplines, going off cliffs and out into the backcountry where there is always the danger of avalanche. In-line doesn't have a similar history. Skaters go down handrails and into the half-pipe, but they took all that from skateboarding.

"There are people trying to make skating into something different. But it will take a lot of doing. Skateboarding is now a proven sport. It has a history. In-line never reached that point because it hasn't had enough of its own direction."

BMX champ Rick Thorne believes that in-line is a "cheaper" version of skateboarding, but acknowledges that the top skaters demonstrate real skill.

"There just aren't as many in-line skaters competing in the real tough stuff now," Thorne says. "It's a smaller group, though they still have magazines and contests. To tell you the truth, some of the tricks in-line skaters are doing now on vert I wouldn't do. It's pretty gnarly stuff. Some really serious, sick stuff is being done on vert."

It is never easy to compare one sport to another. Some say hitting a baseball is the most difficult thing to master in all of sports. But does that make baseball a more difficult team sport than, say, basketball or hockey? Each sport is different. Unfortunately, perhaps, many of the competitions and styles are similar in alternative sports. All have the half-pipe and a street-style. It may be time to acknowledge that the great athletes in in-line skating are every bit as talented as those in other sports, but the way Jon Julio sees it, it may require more participants, creating an in-line history of their own.

"There are more young people coming in, so you often have a new star or see a new trick, tempting you to attain the next level," Julio said. "But at this point in time with in-line, there are more street and hardcores, and not too many people know about them. With vert contests and events such as my IMYTA contests, I hope we will bring our sport to a national audience, so more people can see it and understand where it's heading. There are so many talented kids and creative minds in the sport now. As they mature and receive more exposure, the sport will grow."

Probably, Julio is right. With the advent of talented young athletes who want to try new things, and with increased exposure through the X-Games and other contests, new people will join the sport and it will grow. The top two vert skaters in the world may now be from Japan, but their tricks and maneuvers will be seen and copied by young American skaters. Very likely, we will see the same kind of evolution that has shaped the other sports. For example, once Tony Hawk and Dave Mirra came to prominence, skateboarding and BMXing began to grow. Likewise, vert skating is exciting to watch and the top athletes are sensational. If the exposure continues, and one or two superstars emerge, the sport can only expand.

## Flying High

Undoubtedly, if skaters in the half-pipe get more exposure the crowds will come. Jon Julio has talked about a pair of Japanese brothers "who are doing extraordinary things in the pipe, going fourteen feet in the air."

He wasn't kidding. Takeshi Yasutoko, 16, and his brother Eito, 19, finished first and second in aggressive vert at the 2002 X-Games, blowing away the rest of the field. The brothers appear to be skaters who know no bounds.

"If ever there was an example of how little conditioning and strength has to do with success in in-line skating, it is young Takeshi Yasutoko," said veteran skater Arlo Eisenberg. "He was the youngest vert skater to win a medal at the X-Games and his success is a testament to the importance of technique and confidence over conditioning and strength."

Eisenberg doesn't mean that Yasutoko was out of shape. But at a mere 5'3" and 110 pounds, he is a small man and by no means among the strongest. At 5'8" and 143 pounds, Eito Yasutoko is somewhat bigger, but no less dynamic. He has twice won X-Games gold medals in vert, in 1999 and 2000, and is known for raising tricks to new standards, as well as for trying tricks no one else dares. A perfect example was his 1440 flat spin (four full revolutions in which the body is horizontal in the air). Can you imagine how much air a skater must catch to do that? He has to fly very high.

The brothers come from a family known as the "first skate family of Japan," in which every member has been skating most of their lives. The brothers have always spurred each other on to greater heights. Their father, Yuki Yasutoko says "Takeshi is a good skater because of his brother, Eito. They are healthy rivals, pushing each other to be better skaters and to be number one."

There are other fine skaters on the circuit now, as well. Marc Englehart of Sellersville, Pennsylvania, placed third in the vert event at the 2002 X-Games, behind the brothers. Even at age 19, Englehart is considered a late bloomer who also followed in the footsteps of a brother (Andre). Before the games, he said he would "like to finish in the top five." He discovered he could do better than that.

Also at the X-Games that year, Jaren Grob of Provo, Utah, was the winner in aggressive park skating. He has been a world champion in streetstyle and his aggressive way of skating has led to the nickname "The Monster." He's known for big, burly stunts, such as huge 900s, and he has an attitude typical of those in alternative sports.

"It's all very simple," Jaren has said. "You show up to the course, spend very little time thinking about your run, just get out there and do it, then look for the girls."

The women's aggressive park champion the same year was Martina Svobodova from Slovakia, a former world champion and a hardcore street skater whose strength is in skating rails. She rivals Fabiola Da Silva of São

Paulo, Brazil, who is widely considered the best female in-line skater in the world.

"I think Fabiola is a great skater," Martina said. "She is the best girl in vert, and on street she is good at transfers and transitions, which I am not so good at. But I think I am better at rails."

Apparently, Fabiola is ready for any challenge. With vert contests for women not currently held, she is fully prepared to compete against men and win in a unisex format. "I can't give up," she has said. "I believe that girls can do it and I am going to keep skating and trying my hardest. In the beginning it will be difficult, but in the future it's going to be good."

Will the future be good? With continued TV exposure and fans copying the great vert tricks they see being done, the sport may again take its place among the top alternative disciplines. Mike Budnik, who at age 28, is one of the oldest competitors on the circuit, skating since 1987, believes that the future is in vert.

"Vert skating is so much more exciting to me now than what's going on in street," he said. "Everyone in vert right now is going so big, with the craziest tricks I have seen in a while."

Ironically, as is the case with BMX riding, it's the hardcores who keep the sport alive, especially during its down periods. The high-flyers may get most of the attention and win most of the money, but the down-in-the-dirt hardcores will build the sport and attract many of the new competitors. Yet there is no question that catching air is still the sport's biggest draw.

Matt Lindemuth, 22, is a vert skater who has been competing since 1994. He still gets a thrill from the kind of skating he does.

"You can't describe the rush," Lindemuth has said. "Get some skates and get some air on a half-pipe is all I can say. It's faster and flows much more than street or park."

Like so many who fall in love with these sports, Lindemuth would like to stay involved for a long time. When his competitive days are over, he would like to start an in-line company to remain a part of the industry. Like Jon Julio, Lindemuth admits that his sport has some catching up to do.

"Skateboarding and BMX biking have been given more coverage than in-line, but I hope things will change. Ours is a fairly new sport and we've gone through our growing pains."

Typical of the future of in-line skating is Deborah West, who was already a touring pro in 2001 at age fifteen. An up-and-coming force in park skating, she has picked up several sponsors and spent a great deal of time away from her home in Plano, Texas. And she's already competing against boys.

"I love it," she said. "Guys push my limits and make me skate harder."

With attitudes like hers, young athletes cannot help but improve and excel. Jon Julio has predicted that more and more young athletes will turn to in-line, starting early, and will shape the sport's future in the way he feels it deserves.

"When I was young I would try everything," he said. "Young skaters today have videos that show just how high the level has become. Like I said, they want to learn fast. The prize money has gone up during the past couple of years. It's not the equal of snowboarding or skateboarding, but at venues such as the X-Games it's getting close. When the talented kids who are emerging today get older and get more exposure, the sport will grow."

Another vehicle that will help bring in-line skating closer to the other alternative sports is a new video game called Aggressive Inline. Developed by the same team that worked on Dave Mirra's freestyle BMX game, it has been billed as the first authentic aggressive in-line skating game. Aggressive Inline features ten top professional skaters, and allows players to "be" one of their favorite stars as they explore and master a fully-interactive array of pedestrians, traffic systems, and outrageous gravity-defying challenges.

The complex game offers ten to fifteen cinematic events per level, each with thirty to sixty objectives, accompanied by a soundtrack including several well-known bands. Seven huge levels serve up a variety of ramps, rails, pipes, and other surprises, similar to games created for skateboarding and BMX. As one reviewer commented, "Aggressive Inline is a success. The large number of goals in the game vary in difficulty, giving newer players something to do while not skimping on the difficulty. Fans of Tony Hawk and Dave Mirra will find a lot to like."

This is a sport on the rise. And with millions of recreational skaters nationwide, it will take only a handful of young skaters here and there to decide to cross over—to realize that aggro or streetstyle is for them—and the sport will make giant strides. Like the other sports celebrated in these pages, the future of in-line skating appears bright.

# Conclusion

The influence of the ESPN X-Games continues to be a factor in the growth of alternative sports. ESPN has recently teamed up with Woodward Camp, the Mills Corporation, and Burroughs & Chapin Company to create the first-ever X-Games Skate Parks. The parks are located at four Mills properties: Discover in Atlanta, Franklin in Philadelphia, Grapevine in Dallas, and the newest park, Colorado Mills in Denver.

The parks offer public facilities for skateboarding, BMX stunt riding, and in-line skating, all in a world-class facility designed to offer an authentic X-Games experience. The park at Colorado Mills is a 40,000-square-foot facility that includes an 18,000 square foot street course, three vert ramps, a spin, a bowl, and a beginner street course. The ramps range from beginner to pro, and each park offers instructional sessions in all disciplines. Skateboarders and in-liners share the facilities during session hours and separate sessions for BMX riders are available throughout the week.

The outlets for these sports are on the rise. The hardcore riders continue to take to the streets, the mainstreamers enter the contests, and more facilities are opening to attract new participants and encourage others to higher achievements. With these sports being enjoyed by second and third generations of riders, more parents are supporting their children's efforts in alternative sports. In another ten or twenty years, perhaps, ever fewer kids may be playing baseball, football, and basketball, and more kids catching air. Who knows?

If you haven't yet seen the best of the best in these sports, make it your business to watch them. You'll be amazed at the things you see. Here are superb athletes who put their bodies on the line each time they compete, and they are prompting their sports to higher and higher levels of competitiveness and difficulty. *Tricks* may soon be too mild a word for what these athletes do. They are executing complex gymnastic and aerial maneuvers which frequently defy description or category, and are almost beyond belief.

Sometimes it seems that these athletes are not only catching air, but are riding their boards, bikes, and skates ever upward, twisting and turning their way to the skies before they land, a smile on their faces and the rush of achievement in their hearts. Watch them perform only once and you'll see that they love every minute of it.

# Index

Note: Page numbers in *italics* indicate illustrations.